VERY BRITISH BABY KNITS

30 stylish designs fit for a royal baby

by Susan Campbell

SEARCH PRESS

Contents

Project Gallery

Anmer Overalls
page 18

Anmer Sweater
page 21

Anmer Cardigan
page 24

Anmer Hooded Top
page 28

Anmer Hat
page 32

Anmer Booties
page 34

Anmer Bunny Overalls
page 36

Balmoral Dress
page 40

Balmoral Cardigan
page 42

Balmoral Sweater
page 46

Balmoral Headband
page 50

Balmoral Shoes
page 52

Balmoral Bunny Dress &
Headband *page 54*

Highgrove Crossover Cardigan
page 58

Highgrove Sweater
page 60

Highgrove Pants
page 62

Highgrove Hat
page 64

Highgrove Booties
page 66

Highgrove Bunny Sweater & Pants *page 70*

Sandringham Cardigan
page 74

Sandringham Overalls
page 78

Sandringham Sweater
page 80

Sandringham Hat
page 84

Sandringham Booties
page 86

Sandringham Bunny Overalls
page 88

Windsor All-in-one
page 92

Windsor Cabled Sweater
page 96

Windsor Cardigan
page 99

Windsor Hat
page 102

Windsor Booties
page 104

Windsor Bunny All-in-one
page 106

Toy Bunnies
page 110

KENSINGTON PALACE

January 7th 1990.

Dear Mrs Campbell, It was so

K...
se...
h...

& all the best for your
family & friends for 1990.
Yours most sincerely,
Diana.

Mrs B. Campbell.
Sedgeford Hall.
Hunstanton,
Norfolk PE36 5LT

My drawing ro...
it was so nice to see... the Hu... ...bell
...D swimming pool & to hear about the ...   Diana...
shoes from Charlie — lots of love from,   Sedgeford Hall.
Hunstanton,
NOR...

INTRODUCTION

I live and work in a wonderful valley in northwest Norfolk, an area rather grandly known as the Royal Coast. Our estate borders on the Royal Sandringham Estate, the country home and traditional Christmas retreat of HRH Queen Elizabeth II and her family. Recently we were delighted to welcome yet more royal neighbours; the Duke and Duchess of Cambridge have refurbished Anmer Hall, which is even closer to us than Sandringham House. Very British Baby Knits has been designed with the new generation of royal children very much in mind.

Being a mother of six, stepmother of two, grandmother of nine and step-grandmother of ten, I count myself an expert in the grandmother world, and more importantly a veteran in the design of baby clothes. I've been designing small person's knitwear for a very long time – no design of mine will have to be squeezed over a baby's head and no baby will have to be stripped almost naked to facilitate a nappy change.

My baby knitwear designs have travelled far – from angel tops to tank tops, from cot blankets to sleep-bags, from knitted lace to contemporary chunky – a journey that I have enjoyed every stitch of the way.

Any Royal watcher will be in awe of the knitwear sported by the very young Royals – such style, such finish, so classic, so cute and so unobtainable – until now.

My new collection is based unashamedly on classic British design, never boring, never outdated, never fussy, with the added bonus that the designs are quick and easy to knit.

I hope you enjoy knitting my designs for your own 'prince' or 'princess'.

The Collections

Anmer

Balmoral

Highgrove

Sandringham

Windsor

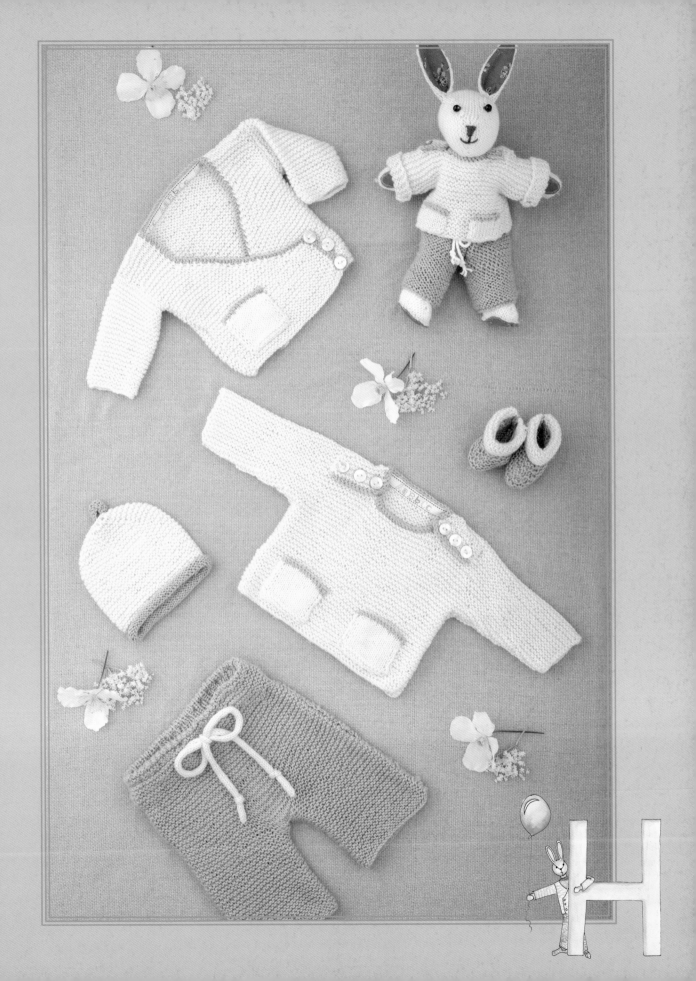

Anmer

Anmer Hall, North West Norfolk, is the country home of the Duchess of Cambridge and two future Kings, Prince William and the adorable Prince George. Built of brick, local carrstone and tile, it has graceful arched windows and sits in glorious countryside. The Anmer collection is typically Catherine – Duchess of Cambridge's style; classic, not 'fussy' and easy to wear but, at the same time modern and trendy. The blue and clay are much favoured colours for the blue-eyed Prince George.

SIZES
Up to 3(3–6:6–9:9–12) months

YARN
Rowan *Baby Merino Silk DK (double knitting) yarn* in Sky 676 and Clay 679

NOTE:
If knitting more than one design the yarn quantities will be reduced for each item, for instance the booties take less than a quarter of a ball of each colour so could easily be knitted from leftovers.

Overalls

SIZES
Up to 3(3–6:6–9:9–12) months

FRONT
Right leg
Using 3.5mm (US 4) needles and CC, cast on
25(26:28:30) sts.
Work 4 rows in garter st.
Change to MC and 4.5mm (US 7) needles and
work in st st until leg measures 10(13:16:19)cm/
4(5:6¼:7½)in, or required length ending on a WS
row. Place sts onto a stitch holder.

Left leg
Work Left front leg the same as Right.

BODY
Next row (RS) K across sts from first leg, cast
on 1 st and K across sts from second leg.
51(53:57:61) sts*
Next row P.
1st size only K24, s2kpo, K24. *49 sts*
Next row P.

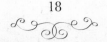

All sizes
Next row K23(25:27:29), s2kpo, K23(25:27:29).
47(51:55:59) sts
Next row P.
Next row K22(24:26:28), s2kpo, K22(24:26:28).
45(49:53:57) sts
Next row P.
Next row K21(23:25:27) s2kpo, K21(23:25:27).
43(47:51:55) sts
Cont straight until front measures 26(31:36:41)cm/
10¼(12¼:14:16¼)in, ending on a WS row.
Change to CC, in garter st work straight for
3cm/1¼in, ending on a WS row.

Front armhole shaping
Cast off 3 sts at beg of next 2 rows, then cast off
2 sts at beg of next 2 rows, then dec 1 st at beg of
next 2(4:4:6) rows. *31(33:37:39) sts***
Cont straight until armhole measures 4.5(5:5:5:6)cm/
1¾(2:2¼:2½)in, ending on a WS row.

Shape for front neck
K9(9:10:10), cast off the centre 13(15:17:19) sts,
K to end.
Work each side separately.
Work 3.5(4:4.5:5)cm/1¼(1½:1¾:2)in straight.
Buttonhole row K2, yf, K2tog, K1(1:2:2), K2tog,
yf, K2.
K 3 rows.
Cast off.
Re-join yarn and work other shoulder to match

BACK
Work as for Front until **.

Back armhole shaping
Cont straight until the back armhole measures
8(9:10:11)cm/3(3½:4:4½)in from armhole shaping,
ending on a WS row.

Back neck shaping
K9(9:10:10), cast off the centre 13(15:17:19) sts,

K to end.
Work each side separately,
Work 2cm/¾in straight.
Cast off.
Re-join yarn and work other shoulder to match.

BUTTON BAND (make one)
Using 3.5mm (US 4) needles and CC, cast on 7 sts.
Slipping the first st in every row, work in garter st until
the band, slightly stretched, is the same length as the
inside legs and gusset.
Cast off.
With pieces of coloured yarn, evenly place
9(10:11:12) markers to indicate the positions of
the buttons.

Buttonhole band
Work as for button band, working a buttonhole to
correspond with each button marker.
Buttonhole row Sl1, K2, yf, K2tog, K2.

TO MAKE UP
Block and press work.
Using mattress stitch, join both side seams.
Join the buttonhole band to the front legs.
Sew the button band to the outside of the back inner
edge, so that it lays flat on the RS of the work.
Sew buttons to correspond with the buttonholes.

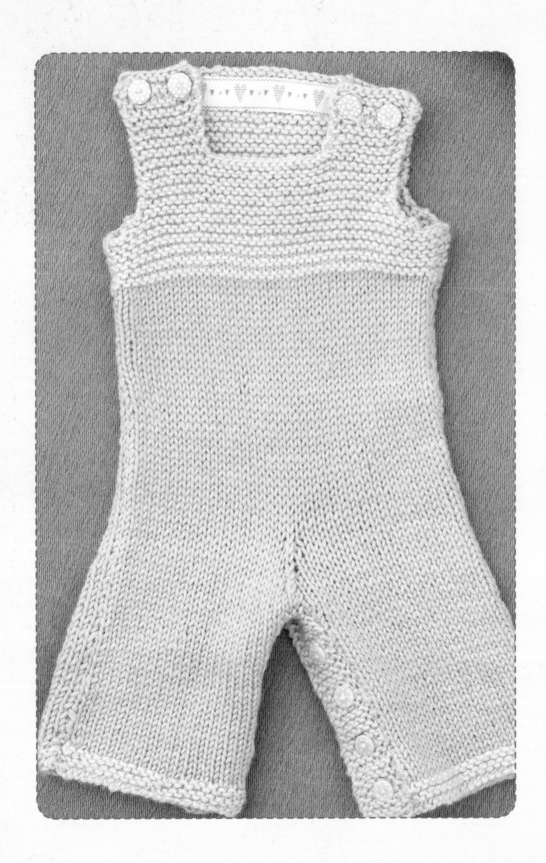

Sweater

You will need

YARN

Rowan *Baby Merino Silk DK*

2(2:2:3) x 50g/1¾oz balls in Sky (MC)

1(1:1:1) x 50g/1¾oz ball in Clay (CC)

NEEDLES

Pair each of 3.5mm (US 4) and 4mm (US 6) knitting needles

Stitch holder

EXTRAS

Buttons: 7 for all sizes

TENSION

22 sts and 44 rows to 10cm/4in square over garter st using 4mm (US 6) needles.

ABBREVIATIONS

See page 124.

NOTE Sweater is worked as a single piece, beginning at the front.

SIZES

Up to 3(3–6:6–9:9–12) months

FRONT

Using 4mm (US 6) needles and CC, cast on 46(52:58:64) sts and work 4 rows in garter st. Change to MC and work in garter st until front measures 11(14:17:19)cm/4¼(5½:6¾:7½)in.

Cast on for sleeves

Inc at each side on every alt row.

1st size Cast on 6 sts, three times, then 4 sts twice. *26 sts per sleeve*

2nd size Cast on 8 sts, three times, then 10 sts once. *34 sts per sleeve*

3rd size Cast on 8 sts, five times. *40 sts per sleeve*

4th size Cast on 10 sts, four times, then 6 sts once. *46 sts per sleeve*

Work straight on the 98(120:138:156) sts until work measures 18(20.5:24:27)cm/7(8:9½:10½)in.

Next row K41(51:59:67), cast off 16(18:20:22) sts from the centre.

Cont on the rem 41(51:59:67) sts.

Work another 8(10:12:12) rows, ending at the neck edge.

Next row *K2, yf, K2tog* rep from * to * twice more, K to end.

K 3 rows more.

Cast off 12 sts.

K to end.

Next row K to end, cast on 12 sts.*

Slip all sts from this side onto a stitch holder.

Re-join yarn and work the second shoulder as the first shoulder to *, reversing shaping.

Next row Cast on 16(18:20:22) sts for the back neck and re-join the sts from the stitch holder, K to end.

Work straight on the 98(120:138:156) sts until work measures 29(32:37:41)cm/11½(12½:14½:16)in.

Cast off to shape the sleeve as foll:

1st size Cast off 4 sts at beg of next 2 rows twice, then cast off 6 sts at beg of next 2 rows three times. *46 sts*

2nd size Cast off 10 sts at beg of next 2 rows once, then 8 sts at beg of next 2 rows, three times. *52 sts*

3rd size Cast off 8 sts at beg of next 2 rows, five times. *58 sts*

4th size Cast off 6 sts at beg of next 2 rows once, then cast off 10 sts at beg of next 2 rows, four times. *64 sts*

Cont on the rem 46(52:58:64) sts until the Back measures the same as the Front to border.

Work 4 rows in CC.

Cast off.

POCKET (make 1)

Using 3.5mm (US 4) needles and MC, cast on 10 sts.

Work 2 rows in garter st.

Beg with a K row, work 8 rows in st st.

Change to CC.

K 1 row.

Cast off.

BORDERS AND EDGES
Button bands
Left neck band

Using 4mm (US 6) needles and CC, with RS of work facing and commencing at the back left neck, pick up and K2 sts.

K 5 rows.

Cast off.

Right neck band

With RS facing, using 4mm (US 6) needles and CC, begin at the right shoulder edge and work as for Left neck band.

Back neck edge

Beg at the right neck edge and with RS of work facing, using 4mm (US 6) needles and CC, pick up and K into every st.

Cast off.

Front neck edge

Beg at the left neck edge and with RS of work facing, using 4mm (US 6) needles and CC, pick up and K into every st.

Cast off.

Sleeve edges

Using 3.5mm (US 4) needles and with RS facing, pick up and K24(28:32:36) sts.

K 3 rows.

Cast off.

TO MAKE UP

Block and press work.

Using mattress stitch, sew the side seams together.

Sew the end of the button bands under the buttonhole band.

Sew buttons opposite the buttonholes.

Sew button onto pocket and sew pocket into place.

Cardigan

You will need

YARN
Rowan *Baby Merino Silk DK*
2(2:2:3) x 50g/1¾oz balls in Sky 676 (MC)
1(1:1:1) x 50g/1¾oz ball in Clay 679 (CC)

NEEDLES
Pair each of 3.25mm (US 3), 3.5mm (US 4) and
4mm (US 6) knitting needles
Stitch holder

EXTRAS
Buttons: 7(9:10:11)

TENSION
20 sts and 28 rows to 10cm/4in square over st st
using 4mm (US 6) needles.

ABBREVIATIONS
See page 124.

SIZES
Up to 3(3–6:6–9:9–12) months

BACK
Using 4mm (US 6) needles and CC, cast on
45(51:57:63) sts and work 2 rows in garter st.
Change to MC and st st and work straight until
work measures 11(13:15:17)cm/4¼(5:6:6¾)in.

Armhole shaping
Cast off 2 sts at beg of next 2 rows.
Row 1 K1, K2tog tbl, K to last 3 sts, K2tog, K1.
Row 2 P.

Rep rows 1 and 2 until 23(25:27:27) sts rem, ending
on a WS row.
Next row K1, sk2po, K to last 4 sts, K3tog, K1.
Next row P.
Rep last 2 rows once more.
Slip rem 15(17:19:19) sts onto a stitch holder.

LEFT FRONT

Using 4mm (US 6) needles and CC, cast on 21(23:27:29) sts and work 2 rows in garter st.

Change to MC and work straight in st st until front measures the same as the back up to the armhole shaping, ending with a WS row.

Shape raglan

Cast off 2 sts at beg of next row.

Work 1 row.

Row 1 K1, K2tog tbl, K to end.

Row 2 P.

Rep rows 1 and 2 until 13(13:16:15) sts rem, ending at the front edge.

Shape neck

Cast off 1(1:2:1) st(s), work to end.

Cont to dec as before on raglan edge, at the same time dec 1 st at the neck edge on next three rows, then the foll 1(1:2:2) alt row(s). *5 sts*

Work 1 row.

Next row K1, sk2po, K1.

Next row P3.

Next row K1, skpo.

Fasten off.

RIGHT FRONT

Using 4mm (US 6) needles and CC, cast on 21(23:27:29) sts and work 2 rows in garter st.

Change to MC and work straight until front measures the same as back to the armhole shaping, ending with a RS row.

Shape raglan

Cast off 2 sts at beg of next row.

Work 2 rows.

Row 1 K to last 3 sts, K2tog, K1.

Row 2 P.

Rep rows 1 and 2 until 13(13:16:15) sts rem, ending at the front edge.

Shape neck

K2(2:3:2)tog, work to last 3 sts, K2tog, K1.

Cont to dec as before on raglan edge, at the same time dec 1 st at the neck edge on next three rows, then the foll 1(1:2:2) alt row(s). *5 sts*

Next row K1, K3tog, K1.

Next row P3.

Next row K2tog, K1.

Fasten off.

SLEEVES

Using 3.25mm (US 3) needles and CC, cast on 29(31:33:35) sts and work 2 rows in garter st.

Change to MC and work 8(12:12:12) rows in st st.

Change to 4mm (US 6) needles and inc 1 st at each end of the next and every foll 6th(4th:6th:6th) row until there are 37(41:45:49) sts, then work 5(7:3:7) rows or until sleeve is the required length.

Shape raglan

Cast off 2 sts at beg of next 2 rows.

Row 1 K1, K2tog tbl, K to last 3 sts, K2tog, K1.

Row 2 P.

Rep rows 1 and 2 until 15(15:15:11) sts rem, ending with a WS row.

Next row K1, sk2po, K to last 4 sts, K3tog, K1. *11(11:11:7) sts.*

Next row P.

1st, 2nd and 3rd sizes only

Rep the last 2 rows until 7 sts rem.

All sizes

Slip sts onto a stitch holder.

POCKETS (make 2)

Using 4mm (US 6) needles and CC, cast on 15(16:18:19) sts and K2 rows.

Change to st st and work until pocket measures 5.5(8:10:11.5)cm/2¼(3¼:4:4½)in.

Cast off.

FRONT BANDS
Button band (make 1)
Using 3.5mm (US 4) needles and CC, cast on
7 sts.
Slipping the first st in every row, work in garter
st until the band, slightly stretched, is the same
length as the front edge.
Cast off.
With pieces of coloured yarn, evenly place
7(9:10:11) markers to indicate the positions of
the buttons.

Buttonhole Band
Work as for button band, working a buttonhole to
correspond with each button marker.
Buttonhole row Sl1, K2, yf, K2tog, K2.

TO MAKE UP
Block and press work.
Join raglans.
Join side and sleeve seams.
Sew bands onto front edges in the appropriate
position, (buttonhole band on left side for a boy and
right side for a girl).

Neck band
Using 3.5mm (US 4) needles and with RS facing, beg
at the right front, K across the 7 sts at the top of the
right band. Pick up and K9(10:11:13) sts from right
side of neck, then K across the 7 sts from top of the
arm, then the 15(17:19:19) sts from back, 7 sts from
second sleeve, pick up and K9(10:11:13) sts from left
side of neck, and K across the 7 sts from the left band.
61(65:69:73) sts
K 2 rows.
Cast off.
Sew pockets into place.
Sew buttons opposite buttonholes.

Hooded Top

You will need

YARN

Rowan *Baby Merino Silk DK*

3(3) x 50g/1¾oz balls in Sky 676 (MC)

Small amount of Clay 679 (CC), for covered buttons

NEEDLES

Pair each of 2.25mm (US 1), 4mm (US 6) and 4.5mm (US 7) knitting needles

3mm (US 2/3) circular needle

Stitch holder

EXTRAS

Buttons: 8 very small buttons, for covering (approx. 1cm/³⁄₈in diameter)

TENSION

24 sts and 32 rows to 10cm/4in square over rice st using 4mm (US 6) needles.

ABBREVIATIONS

Rice st – 1st row: [K1, P1] to end; 2nd row: K to end.

See also page 124.

SIZES

Up to 6(6–12) months

BACK

Using 4mm (US 6) needles, cast on 56(62) sts and working in rice st, work straight until back measures 14(17)cm/5½(6½)in from cast-on edge, ending on a WS row.

Shape raglan

Keeping rice st correct:

Cast off 3 sts at beg of next 2 rows. *50(56) sts*

Next row (RS) K1, K2tog tbl, patt to last 3 sts, K2tog, K1.

Next row K.

Rep the last 2 rows until 20(22) sts rem, ending with a WS row.

Leave rem sts on a stitch holder.

FRONT

Using 4mm (US 6) needles, cast on 56(62) sts and working in rice st throughout, work straight until front measures 4cm/1½in, ending with a WS row.

Next row Keeping rice st correct, work 19(22) sts, cut yarn, slip next 18 sts onto a stitch holder, rejoin yarn and work 19(22) sts.

Next row Work 19(22) sts, placing stitch holder to the RS of the work, cast on 18 sts, work 19(22) sts to end. Work 30 rows. Leave these 56(62) sts on the needle and work the pocket as foll:

Working in rice st and using the sts from the stitch holder, work 32 rows, ending on a WS row.

Next row Return to the sts on the needle, work 19(22) sts, join the 18 sts from the pocket by working one st from the front and one from the pocket, with the next 18 sts from the front, work 19(22) sts to end. Cont in rice st, work straight until front measures 14(17)cm/5½(6½)in from cast-on edge, ending on a WS row.

Shape raglan

Keeping rice st correct:

Cast off 3 sts at beg of next 2 rows. *50(56) sts*

Next row (RS) K1, K2tog tbl, patt to last 3 sts, K2tog, K1.

Next row K.

Rep the last 2 rows until 44(46) sts rem, ending with a WS row.

Divide for front opening

Next row (RS) K1, K2tog tbl, work 17(18) sts, turn, leaving rem sts on a stitch holder and working on 19(20) sts. Cont to work raglan edge, dec on every alt row as before until 8(9) sts rem, ending on a WS row. Leave these sts on a holder.

Slip second side sts onto needles and, with RS facing, cast off centre 4 sts, work to last 3 sts, K2tog, K1. *19(20) sts*

Complete to match first shoulder, reversing shaping ending at centre edge.

Do not break yarn but keep for hood.

SLEEVES (both alike)

Using 4mm (US 6) needles, cast on 30(30) sts and work 4cm/1½in in K1, P1 rib.

Working in rice st throughout, inc 1 st at each end of next and every foll 5th row until there are 42(46) sts. Cont straight until sleeve measures 12(15)cm/4¾(6)in or required length, ending with a WS row.

Shape raglan

Cast off 3 sts at beg of next 2 rows. *36(40) sts*

Next row (RS) K1, K2tog tbl, patt to last 3 sts, K2tog, K1.

Next row K.

Rep the last 2 rows until 6(6) sts rem, ending with a WS row.

Leave rem sts on a stitch holder.

HOOD

With RS facing, using 4mm (US 6) needles and commencing at yarn left unbroken, K across 8(9) sts from right front, 6(6) sts from top of sleeve, 20(22) sts from back, 6(6) sts from second sleeve and 8(9) sts from left front. *48(52) sts*

Next row (WS) K5(5), inc into next st, * K1, inc into next st*, rep from * to * to last 6(6) sts, K to end. *67(73) sts*

Cont straight, working in rice st throughout until hood measures 13(14)cm/5(5½)in from neck edge, ending on a WS row.

Shape crown

Place a stitch marker on the 34th(37th) st of the last row.

Next row (RS) Keeping rice st correct, work to within 2 sts of marker, K2tog, K1(marked st), K2tog tbl, work to end.

Next row K.

Rep last 2 rows twice more. *61(67) sts*

Next row (RS) Keeping rice st correct, work to within 2 sts of marker, K2tog, K1 (marked st), K2tog tbl, work to end.

Next row K to within 2 sts of marker, K2tog tbl, K1 (marked st), K2tog, work to end.

Rep the last 2 rows twice more. *49(55) sts*

Cast off.

Using mattress stitch, join the top of the hood

BANDS

Using 3mm (US 2/3) circular needle and with RS facing, begin at the base of the front opening, and pick up and K18 sts up the right of the front opening. Then pick up and K42(44) sts evenly up to the top seam then K42(44) sts evenly up to the neck and 18 sts from the left front opening. *120(124) sts*

Next row K.

Buttonhole row (girl's version) K6 sts, wrap yarn around needle twice, K2tog, K6, wrap yarn around needle twice, K2tog, K to end.

Buttonhole row (boy's version) K to last 16 sts, wrap yarn around needle twice, K2tog, K6, wrap yarn around needle twice, K2tog, K to end.

K 3 rows more, dropping one of each wrap twice on first row.

Cast off.

TO MAKE UP

Block and press work.

Using mattress stitch, join the raglans together then the sleeve and the side seams.

Pocket bands (work both the same)

With RS facing and using 4mm (US 6) needles, pick up and K13 sts from side of pocket.

K 3 rows.

Buttonhole row K2, *yf, K2tog, K2*, rep from * to *, yf, K2tog, K1.

K 2 rows.

Cast off loosely using a 4.5mm (US 7) needle.

To make the covered buttons (make 8)

Using 2.25mm (US 1) needles, cast on 7 sts and work 9 rows in st st.

Cast off.

Place the button in the centre on the WS of the knitted square (A).

Using small running stitches and strong thread, gather around the button and pull thread tight, fasten off (B).

Sew a couple of stitches through the centre of the button to keep the covering in place (C).

Make a 'stalk' on the underside of the button by wrapping thread around the base (D).

Sew the buttonhole band over the button band at the neck opening and sew the ends of the pocket bands into place.

Sew buttons to correspond with the buttonholes.

MAKING COVERED BUTTONS

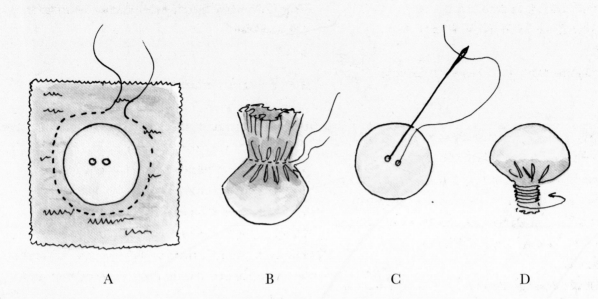

A   B   C   D

Hat

You will need

YARN

Rowan *Baby Merino Silk DK*

1(1:1:1) x 50g/1¾oz ball in Sky 676 (MC)

1(1:1:1) x 50g/1¾oz ball in Clay 679 (CC)

NEEDLES

Pair of 4mm (US 6) knitting needles

TENSION

20 sts and 28 rows to 10cm/4in square over st st using 4mm (US 6) needles.

ABBREVIATIONS

See page 124.

SIZES

Up to 3(3–6:6–9:9–12) months

HAT

Using 4mm (US 6) needles and CC, cast on 56(62:68:68) sts and work 4(4:5:5)cm/1½(1½:2:2)in in garter st.

Change to MC and st st and work straight until work measures 8(10:12:14)cm/3(4:4¾:5½)in from the beg, ending with WS row.

Shape crown

Row 1 K1, *K2tog, K7(8:9:9)*, rep from * to * 6 times, K1.

Work 3 rows.

Row 5 K1, *K2tog, K6(7:8:8)*, rep from * to * 6 times, K1.

Row 6 P.

Row 7 K1, *K2tog, K5(6:7:7)*, rep from * to * 6 times, K1.

Row 8 P.

Row 9 K1, *K2tog, K4(5:6:6)*, rep from * to * 6 times, K1.

Row 10 P.

Row 11 K1, *K2tog, K3(4:5:5)*, rep from * to * 6 times, K1.

Row 12 P.

2nd size only K1, *K2tog, K3*, rep from * to * 6 times, K1.

Next row P.

3rd and 4th sizes only K1, *K2tog, K4(4)*, rep from * to * 6 times, K1.

Next row P.

3rd and 4th sizes only K1, *K2tog, K3(3)*, rep from * to * 6 times, K1.

Next row P.

All sizes

Next row (RS) K1, *K2tog, rep from * to last st, K1.

Next row P.

Next row (RS) K1, *K2tog, rep from * to last st, K1.

Next row P.

Thread yarn through sts and fasten off.

TO MAKE UP

Block and press work.

Join the back seam, inverting the seam for the garter st turnover.

Booties

You will need

YARN

Rowan *Baby Merino Silk DK*

1(1:1:1) x 50g/1¾oz ball in Clay 679 (MC)

1(1:1:1) x 50g/1¾oz ball in Sky 676 (CC)

NEEDLES

Pair of 4mm (US 6) knitting needles

TENSION

22 sts and 38 rows to 10cm/4in square over garter st using 4mm (US 6) needles.

ABBREVIATIONS

See page 124.

SIZES

Up to 3(3–6:6–9:9–12) months

BOOTIES (make 2)

Beg at the sole, using 4mm (US 6) needles and MC, cast on 27(31:35:39) sts.

Work 2 rows in garter st.

Inc on every alt row as foll:

1st row K1, M1 by picking up the loop between sts, K12(14:16:18), M1 as before, K1, M1, K12(14:16:18), M1, K1, K31(35:39:43).

Next row K.

Next row K2, M1, K12(14:16:18), M1, K3, M1, K12(14:16:18), M1, K2. *35(39:43:47) sts*

K 1(3:5:7) row(s).

Next row K14(16:18:20), K2tog, K3, K2tog, K14(16:18:20).

Next row K.

Next row K14(16:18:20), K2tog, K1, K2tog, K14(16:18:20).

Next row K.

Next row K13(15:17:19), K2tog, K1, K2tog, K13(15:17:19).

Next row K.

Next row K12(14:16:18), K2tog, K1, K2tog, K12(14:16:18).

Cont to dec either side of centre toe st on every alt row until there are 21(23:25:27) sts on the needle. Change to CC and K for 4(5:5:6)cm/1½(2:2:2¼)in. Cast off.

TO MAKE UP
Block and press work.
Join the sole with a flat seam.
Join the back seam, inverting the seam at the top for the turnover.

Bunny Overalls

FINISHED SIZE
Length approx. 17cm/6¾in

LEGS (make 2)
Using 3.5mm (US 4) needles and CC, cast on 32 sts using the thumb method, leaving a very long end (this will be used to knit the second band).
K 1 row.

Row 1 K3 in CC, K to last 3 sts in MC, K3 in CC.
Row 2 K3 in CC, P to last 3 sts in MC, K3 in CC.
Rep last 2 rows 9 times more.
Next row Cast off the 3 contrast sts, K to last 3 sts in MC, cast off the 3 CC sts.

Join legs for body
Slip first leg onto needle, then slip second leg onto needle.

Next row P26, inc in last st, P26. *53 sts*

Next row (RS) K25, s2kpo, K to end. *51 sts*

Next row P.

Next row (RS) K24, s2kpo, K to end. *49 sts*

Next row P.

Next row (RS) K23, s2kpo, K to end. *47 sts*

Next row P.

Next row (RS) K22, s2kpo, K to end. *45 sts*

Next row P.

Work 6 rows in st st.

Next row (RS) Change to CC and garter st, and K 7 rows in garter st.

Next row K10, cast off 2 sts, K18, cast off 2 sts, K9. Work on the last 10 sts first.

Next row K8, K2tog.

Next row K.

Next row K7, K2tog.

K 7 rows straight, ending with a WS row.

Cast off 4 sts from back edge. *4 sts*

Work 6 rows.

Cast off.

Slip centre 19 sts onto a stitch holder.

Re-join yarn and work the rem 10 sts as for the first shoulder, reversing the shaping.

Slip the central sts back onto the needle.

Next row (RS) Re-join yarn, K2tog, K to last 2 sts, K2tog.

Next row K.

Rep last 2 rows twice more. *13 sts*

Next row K4, cast off 5 sts, K3.

Work each shoulder separately.

First shoulder

K 1 row.

Buttonhole row K2, yf, K2. 5 sts

Next row K.

Cast off.

Work second shoulder as first.

TO MAKE UP

Block and press work.

Join back seam, leaving an opening for the tail.

Overlap the back leg border with the front leg border, space 8 buttons evenly and sew into place.

Sew a button to the back shoulder straps.

Balmoral

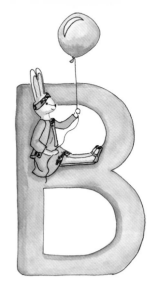

Balmoral Castle was built for Queen Victoria and Prince Albert around 1854 and is very much in the 'Scottish' castle style. Its towers and castellations look as though they have stepped straight out of a child's fairy story. Victoria and Albert's romance blossomed here and the castle is still the Royal family's private home; this is where they stay for up to two months every autumn, when the surrounding landscape is filled with soft, mellow colours. The Balmoral collection is unashamedly romantic, with a smattering of tiny flowers and colours that blend with the prolific Scottish heathers that surround the castle. This is a truly pretty collection.

SIZES
Up to 3(3–6:6–9:9–12) months

YARN
Rowan *Pure Wool 4 ply Baby yarn* in Shell 468 and Porcelaine 451

NOTE:
If knitting more than one design the yarn quantities will be reduced for each item, for instance the booties take less than a quarter of a ball of each colour so could easily be knitted from leftovers.

Dress

YARN

Rowan *Pure Wool 4 ply*

2(2:2:3) x 50g/1¾oz balls in Shell 468 (MC)

Small amount of Porcelaine 451 (CC), for edging and flowers

Scraps of yarn for flower centres

NEEDLES

Pair each of 3mm (US 2/3) and 3.5mm (US 4) knitting needles

EXTRAS

Buttons: 4 for all sizes

TENSION

26 sts and 35 rows to 10cm/4in square over st st using 3.5mm (US 4) needles.

ABBREVIATIONS

See page 124.

SIZES

Up to 3(3–6:6–9:9–12) months

FRONT

Using 3.5mm (US 4) needles and CC, cast on 88(94:100:106) sts.

Work 2 rows in garter st.

Change to MC.

Beg with a K row, change to st st and work 6(8:10:10) rows.

Next row (dec row) K21(23:25:27), s2kpo, K40(42:44:46), s2kpo, K rem 21(23:25:27) sts. Work 5(7:9:11) rows.

Next dec row K20(22:24:26), s2kpo, K38(40:42:44), s2kpo, K rem 20(22:24:26) sts. Work 5(7:9:11) rows.

Next dec row K19(21:23:25), s2kpo, K36(38:40:42), s2kpo, K rem 19(21:23:25) sts.

Work 5(7:9:11) rows.

Next dec row K18(20:22:24), s2kpo, K34(36:38:40), s2kpo, K rem 18(20:22:24) sts.

Cont in this manner, dec in every 6th row until there are 52(58:64:70) sts on the needle.

Work straight until front measures 18(22:25:28)cm/ 7(8¾:9¾:11)in, ending on a WS row.

Shape armholes

Cast off 3 sts at beg of next 2 rows.

Cast off 2 sts at beg of next 2 rows.

Then dec 1 st at beg of every row until 38(42:46:52) sts are on the needles**.

Work straight until armhole measures 6(6:7:8)cm/ 2½(2½:2¾:3¼)in, ending on a WS row.

Shape for neck

K15(17:18:21), cast off 8(8:10:10) sts, K to end.

Work each shoulder separately.

First shoulder

Dec 1 st on every row at the neck edge until 8(9:10:11) sts rem.

Work straight until front armhole measures 11(12:13:14)cm/4¼(4¾:5:5½)in.

Cast off.

Work the second shoulder as for the first.

BACK

Work as for Front to **.

Work straight until armhole measures 8(8:9:10)cm/ 3¼(3¼:3½:4)in, ending on a WS row.

Shape for neck

K15(17:18:21), cast off 8(8:10:10) sts, K to end.

Work each shoulder separately.

First shoulder

Dec 1 st on every row at the neck edge until 8(9:10:11) sts rem.

Work straight until back armhole measures 13(14:15:16)cm/5(5½:6:6¼)in, ending on a WS row.

Buttonhole row K2, yf, K2tog, K0(1:2:3), K2tog, yf, K2.

Work 2 rows.

Cast off.

Work the second shoulder as for the first.

TO MAKE UP

Block and press work.

Sew side seams together.

Left armhole

Using 3mm (US 2/3) needles, with RS facing and CC, beg at the neck edge of the buttonhole band and ending at the neck edge of the button band, K into every st.

Cast off.

Right armhole

Using 3mm (US 2/3) needles, with RS facing and CC, beg at the neck edge of the button band and ending at the neck edge of the buttonhole band, K into every st.

Cast off.

Front neck

Using 3mm (US 2/3) needles, with RS facing and CC, K into every st.

Cast off.

Back neck

Using 3mm (US 2/3) needles, with RS facing and CC, K into every st.

Cast off.

Working in CC and using lazy daisy stitch (see page 123), work a group of flowers on the left shoulder and the lower left skirt.

Place a French knot (see page 123), in the middle of each flower.

Cardigan

You will need

YARN

Rowan *Pure Wool 4 ply*

2(2:2:3) x 50g/1¾oz balls in Shell 468 (MC)

1(1:1:1) x 50g/1¾oz ball in Porcelaine 451 (CC), for edging and flowers

Scraps of yarn for flower centres

NEEDLES

Pair each of 3mm (US 2/3) and 3.5mm (US 4) knitting needles

Stitch holder

EXTRAS

Buttons: 3 for all sizes

TENSION

26 sts and 35 rows to 10cm/4in square over st st using 3.5mm (US 4) needles.

ABBREVIATIONS

See page 124.

SIZES

Up to 3(3–6:6–9:9–12) months

BACK

Using 3.5mm (US 4) needles and CC, cast on 58(62:68:76) sts and work 2 rows in garter st. Change to MC and work straight in st st until back measures 11(13:15:17)cm/4¼(5:6:6¾)in, ending on a WS row.

Raglan shaping

Cast off 2 sts at beg of next 2 rows.

1st and 2nd sizes only

Next row K2, K2tog, K to last 4 sts, K2tog tbl, K2.

Next row P.

Next row K2, K2tog, K to last 4 sts, K2tog tbl, K2.

Next row P.

Next row K2, K3tog, K to last 5 sts, K3tog tbl, K2.

Next row P.

Rep last 6 rows until 18(18) sts rem. Slip sts onto a stitch holder.

3rd size only

Next row K2, K2tog, K to last 4 sts, K2tog tbl, K2.

Next row P.

Next row K2, K2tog, K to last 4 sts, K2tog tbl, K2.

Next row P.

Next row K2, K2tog, K to last 4 sts, K2tog tbl, K2.

Next row P.

Next row K2, K3tog, K to last 5 sts, K3tog tbl, K2.

Next row P.

Rep last 8 rows until 22 sts rem.

Slip sts onto a stitch holder.

4th size only

Next row K2, K2tog, K to last 4 sts, K2tog tbl, K2.

Next row P.

Next row K2, K2tog, K to last 4 sts, K2tog tbl, K2.

Next row P.

Next row K2, K2tog, K to last 4 sts, K2tog tbl, K2.

Next row P.

Next row K2, K3tog, K to last 5 sts, K3tog tbl, K2.

Next row P.

Rep last 8 rows until 30 sts rem.

Next row K2, K2tog, K to last 4 sts, K2tog tbl, K2.

Next row P.

Next row K2, K3tog, K to last 5 sts, K3tog tbl, K2.

Next row P.

Slip 24 sts onto a stitch holder.

FRONTS

(Both alike to armhole shaping)

Using 3.5mm (US 4) needles and CC, cast on 30(32:35:39) sts and work 2 rows in garter st.

Change to MC and work straight in st st until front measures 11(13:15:17)cm/4¼(5:6:6¾)in.

Left side raglan shaping

Beg on a RS row, cast off 2 sts (armhole edge) at beg of row.

Next row P.

1st and 2nd sizes only

Next row K2, K2tog, K to end.

Next row P.

Next row K2, K2tog, K to end.

Next row P.

Next row K2, K3tog, K to end.

Next row P.

Rep last 6 rows until 12(13) sts rem, ending at front edge.

3rd and 4th sizes only

Next row K2, K2tog, K to end.

Next row P.

Next row K2, K2tog, K to end.

Next row P.

Next row K2, K2tog, K to end.

Next row P.

Next row K2, K3tog, K to end.

Next row P.

Rep last 8 rows until 15(16) sts rem, ending at front edge.

All sizes

Shape neck

Next row Cont shaping the raglan as before but dec 1 st on alt rows, cast off 4(5:7:8) sts at the neck edge.

Work 1 row.

Next row Cast off 2 sts at neck edge.

Cont with the raglan shaping until 4 sts rem.

P2tog twice.

Fasten off.

Right raglan shaping

Beg on a WS row, cast off 2 sts at beg of row (armhole edge).

Work 2 rows.

1st and 2nd sizes only

Next row K to last 4 sts, K2tog tbl, K2.

Next row P.

Next row K to last 4 sts, K2tog tbl, K2.

Next row P.

Next row K to last 5 sts, K3tog tbl, K2.

Next row P.

Rep last 6 rows until 12(13) sts rem, ending at front edge.

3rd and 4th sizes only

Next row K to last 4 sts, K2tog tbl, K2.

Next row P.

Next row K to last 4 sts, K2tog tbl, K2.

Next row P.

Next row K to last 4 sts, K2tog tbl, K2.

Next row P.

Next row K to last 5 sts, K3tog tbl, K2.

Next row P.

Rep last 8 rows until 15(16) sts rem, ending at front edge.

All sizes

Shape neck

Next row Cont shaping the raglan as before but dec 1 st on alt rows, cast off 4(5:7:8) sts at the neck edge.

Work 1 row.

Next row Cast off 2 sts at neck edge, cont with raglan shaping until 4 sts rem.

P2tog twice.

Fasten off.

SLEEVES

Using 3.5mm (US 4) needles and CC, cast on 38(40:42:44) sts and work 2 rows in garter st.

Change to MC and work straight in st st, inc 1 st at each of every 12th row, until 42(46:50:54) sts rem.

Work straight until sleeve measures 10(12:15:18)cm/ 4(4¾:6:7)in, ending on a WS row.

Cast off 2(2:2:1) st(s) at beg of next 2 rows.

Next row K2, K2tog, K to last 4 sts, K2tog tbl, K2.

Next row P.

Rep last 2 rows until 10(12:12:14) sts rem.

Slip sts onto a stitch holder.

TO MAKE UP

Block and press work, making sure the raglans are blocked to an even length.

Join raglan seams.

Join side and sleeve seams.

Neck and front bands worked all in one

Using 3mm (US 2/3) needles and CC, with RS facing and beg at the lower right front, pick up and K into every st to the neck edge, then pick up 14(16:18:20) sts from right side of neck, then K10(12:12:14) sts from top of sleeve stitch holder, K18(18:22:24) sts from back stitch holder, K10(12:12:14) sts from top of second sleeve stitch holder, then pick up and K14(16:18:20) sts from left side of neck, pick up and K into every st on the left front opening.

Cast off.

Make 3 loops on the right front opening.

Sew buttons to correspond with the loops.

Using lazy daisy stitch (see page 123), embroider clusters of flowers with French knot centres (see page 123).

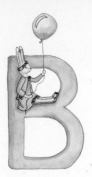

Sweater

YARN

Rowan *Pure Wool 4 ply*

2(2:2:3) x 50g/1¾oz balls in Shell 468 (MC)

1(1:1:1) x 50g/1¾oz ball in Porcelaine 451 (CC), for edging and flowers

Scraps of yarn for flower centres

NEEDLES

Pair each of 3mm (US 2/3) and 3.5mm (US 4) knitting needles

Stitch holder

EXTRAS

Buttons: 5 for all sizes

TENSION

26 sts and 35 rows to 10cm/4in square over st st using 3.5mm (US 4) needles.

ABBREVIATIONS

See page 124.

SIZES

Up to 3(3–6:6–9:9–12) months

BACK

Using 3.5mm (US 4) needles and CC, cast on 58(62:68:76) sts and work 2 rows in garter st. Change to MC and work straight in st st until back measures 11(13:15:17)cm/4¼(5:6:6¾)in ending on a WS row.

Raglan shaping

Cast off 2 sts at beg of next 2 rows.

1st and 2nd sizes only

Next row K2, K2tog, K to last 4 sts, K2tog tbl, K2.

Next row P.

Next row K2, K2tog, K to last 4 sts, K2tog tbl, K2.

Next row P.

Next row K2, K3tog, K to last 5 sts, K3tog tbl, K2.

Next row P.

Rep last 6 rows until 18(18) sts rem.

Slip sts onto a stitch holder.

3rd size only

Next row K2, K2tog, K to last 4 sts, K2tog tbl, K2.

Next row P.

Next row K2, K2tog, K to last 4 sts, K2tog tbl, K2.

Next row P.

Next row K2, K2tog, K to last 4 sts, K2tog tbl, K2.

Next row P.

Next row K2, K3tog, K to last 5 sts, K3tog tbl, K2.

Next row P.

Rep last 8 rows until 22 sts rem.

Slip sts onto a stitch holder.

4th size only

Next row K2, K2tog, K to last 4 sts, K2tog tbl, K2.

Next row P.

Next row K2, K2tog, K to last 4 sts, K2tog tbl, K2.

Next row P.

Next row K2, K2tog, K to last 4 sts, K2tog tbl, K2.

Next row P.

Next row K2, K3tog, K to last 5 sts, K3tog tbl, K2.

Next row P.

Rep last 8 rows until 30 sts rem.

Next row K2, K2tog, K to last 4 sts, K2tog tbl, K2.

Next row P.

Next row K2, K3tog, K to last 5 sts, K3tog tbl, K2.

Next row P.

Slip 24 sts onto a stitch holder.

FRONT

Work as for Back, working the raglan shaping in the appropriate size until 28(30:32:36) sts rem.

Next row Still shaping the raglan as before to match Back, work 10(10:10:11) sts, slip 8(10:12:14) sts from centre front onto a stitch holder, work 10(10:10:11) sts. Work each shoulder separately.

Next row Cast off 2 sts at neck edge.

Work 1 row.

Next row Cast off 2(1:2:2) st(s) at neck edge.

Cont with the raglan shaping until 1 st rem.

Fasten off.

Work second shoulder as for the first.

SLEEVES

Using 3.5mm (US 4) needles and CC, cast on 38(40:42:44) sts and work 2 rows in garter st. Change to MC and work straight in st st, inc 1 st at each of every 12th row until there are 42(46:50:54) sts. Work straight until sleeve measures 10(12:15:18)cm/ 4(4¾:6:7)in or required length, ending on a WS row.

Raglan shaping

Cast off 2(2:2:1) st(s) at beg of next 2 rows.

Next row K2, K2tog, K to last 4 sts, K2tog tbl.

Next row P.

Rep last 2 rows until 10(12:12:14) sts rem.

Slip sts onto a stitch holder.

TO MAKE UP

Block and press work.

Join all the raglans together except the left front raglan, which should be left open.

Neck band

Using 3mm (US 2/3) needles and CC, with RS facing and beg at the left neck edge, pick up and K8(9:10:11) sts from left front neck, K the 8(10:12:14) sts from centre front stitch holder, pick up and K8(9:10:11) sts from right front neck, K the 10(12:12:14) sts from sleeve top stitch holder and 18(18:22:24) sts from back, K the 10(12:12:14) sts from second sleeve. *62(70:78:88) sts*

K 2 rows.

Cast off.

Buttonhole band

Using 3mm (US 2/3) needles and CC, with RS facing and beg 5cm/2in from the left underarm edge, pick up and K23(27:31:35) sts along front raglan edge.

Buttonhole row K3(3:5:5)*, yf, K2tog, K2(3:3:4)*, rep from * to* 3 times, yf, K2tog, K to end.

Cast off.

Sew the sleeve and side seams together.

Sew the left raglan as far as the beg of the buttonhole band.

Sew the button band into place over the raglan.

Sew buttons opposite the buttonholes.

Using lazy daisy stitch (see page 123), embroider clusters of flowers with French knot centres (see page 123).

Headband

You will need

YARN

Rowan *Pure Wool 4 ply*

1(1:1:1) x 50g/1¾oz ball in Shell 468 (MC)

1(1:1:1) x 50g/1¾oz ball in Porcelaine 451 (CC), for edging and flowers

Scraps of yarn for flower centres

NEEDLES

Pair each of 3mm (US 2/3) and 3.5mm (US 4) knitting needles

Stitch holder

EXTRAS

Buttons: 2 for all sizes

TENSION

26 sts and 35 rows to 10cm/4in square over st st using 3.5mm (US 4) needles.

ABBREVIATIONS

See page 124.

SIZES

Up to 3(3–6:6–9:9–12) months

HEADBAND

Using 3.5mm (US 4) needles and CC, cast on 82(86:94:98) sts and work 2 rows in garter st.

Change to MC and beg with a K row, work in st st but keeping the first and last 7 sts of every P row in garter st.

Work 2(2:4:4) rows or to width required, ending on a WS row.

Buttonhole row K to last 7 sts, K3, K2tog, yf, K2.

Work 3(3:5:5) rows.

Next row Work as for buttonhole row.

Work 2(2:4:4) rows.

Change to CC and P 1 row.

Cast off knitways.

BUTTON BAND EDGES (both alike)

With RS facing and CC, pick up and K into every st
from the narrow end of the band.
Cast off.

TO MAKE UP

Block and press work.
Sew buttons in place.
Using lazy daisy stitch (see page 123), embroider
clusters of flowers with French knot centres
(see page 123).

Shoes

You will need

YARN

Rowan *Pure Wool 4 ply*

1(1:1:1) x 50g/1¾oz ball in Shell 468 (MC)

Small amount of Porcelaine 451 (CC), for flowers

Scraps of yarn for flower centres

NEEDLES

Pair of 3mm (US 2/3) knitting needles

Stitch holder

EXTRAS

Buttons: 2 for all sizes

TENSION

23 sts and 39 rows to 10cm/4in square over garter st using 3mm (US 2/3) needles.

ABBREVIATIONS

See page 124.

SIZES

Up to 3(3–6:6–9:9–12) months

SHOES

Using 3mm (US 2/3) needles and MC, cast on 37(41:45:49) sts.

Work 2 rows in garter st.

Row 3 K1, M1, K17(19:21:23), M1, K1, M1, K17(19:21:23), M1, K1. *41(45:49:53) sts*

Row 4 K.

Row 5 K1, M1, K19(21:23:25), M1, K1, M1, K19(21:23:25), M1, K1. *45(49:53:57) sts*

Row 6 K.

Row 7 K22(24:26:28), M1, K1, M1, K22(24:26:28). *47(51:55:59) sts*

Work 5(7:9:11) rows straight.

Next row K21(23:25:27), K2tog tbl, K1, K2tog, K21(23:25:27).

Next row K.

Next row K20(22:24:26), K2tog tbl, K1, K2tog, K20(22:24:26).

Next row K.

Next row K19(21:23:25), K2tog tbl, K1, K2tog, K19(21:23:25).

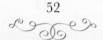

First shoe

Next row K9(11:13:15), cast on 11(13:15:17) sts for the strap, turn and K 1 row on these 20(24:28:32) sts.

Buttonhole row K16(20:24:28), K2tog, yf, K2.

Next row K.

Next row Cast off these 20(24:28:32) sts.

Next row Re-join yarn at beg of strap and cast off 23 sts, K to end.

K 3 rows on the rem 9(11:13:15) sts.

Cast off.

Second shoe

Next row K9(11:13:15), place these sts on a safety pin, cast off 23 sts, then cast on 11(13:15:17) sts for the strap, K to end.

Next row K to last 4 sts, K2tog, yf, K2.

Next row K.

Cast off.

Next row Re-join yarn to the inside edge of the sts on the safety pin.

K 3 rows.

Cast off.

TO MAKE UP

Sew sole with a flat seam.

Sew back seam.

Attach buttons to correspond with the buttonholes.

Embroider a lazy daisy flower (see page 123) in the centre of the shoe upper and sew a French knot (see page 123) in the middle.

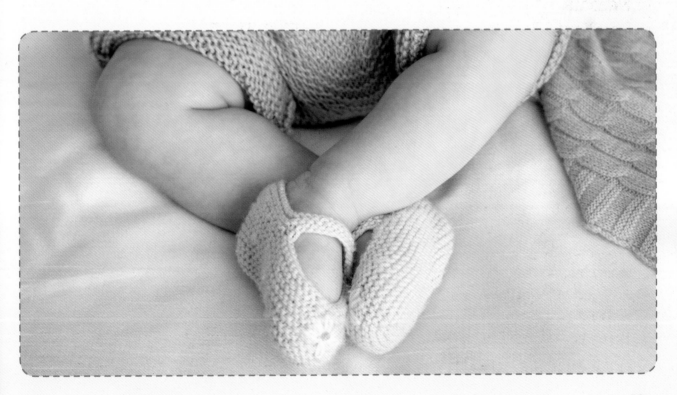

Bunny Dress & Headband

YARN

Rowan *Pure Wool 4 ply*

1(1:1:1) x 50g/1¾oz ball in Shell 468 (MC)

1(1:1:1) x 50g/1¾oz ball in Porcelaine 451 (CC), for edging and flowers

Scraps of yarn for flower centres

NEEDLES

Pair each of 3.5mm (US 4) and 3mm (US 2/3) knitting needles

Stitch holder

EXTRAS

Buttons: 3

TENSION

26 sts and 35 rows to 10cm/4in square over st st using 3.5mm (US 4) needles.

ABBREVIATIONS

See page 124.

FINISHED SIZE

Dress: length approx. 16cm/6¼in

Headband: approx. 18cm/7in diameter

FRONT

Using 3.5mm (US 4) needles and CC, cast on 36 sts and work 2 rows in garter st.

Change to MC and work 4 rows in st st.

Next row K10, s2kpo, K to last 13 sts, s2kpo, K to end.

Work 5 rows in st st.

Next row K9, s2kpo, K to last 12 sts, s2kpo, K to end.

Work 5 rows in st st **.

Next row K8, s2kpo, K to last 11 sts, s2kpo, K to end.

Work 5 rows in st st.

Next row K7, s2kpo, K to last 10 sts, s2kpo, K to end.

Work 5 rows in st st.

Next row K6, s2kpo, K to last 9 sts, s2kpo, K to end. *16 sts.*

Work 5 rows in st st.

Cast off 1 st at beg of next 4 rows. *12 sts.*

Work 5 rows straight.

Next row Work 4, cast off 4 sts, work 4.

Work each shoulder separately by working 4 rows straight on each side. Cast off.

BACK

Work as for Front to **.

Make hole for tail

Next row K8, s2kpo, K3, turn.

Work 4 rows straight on these sts.

Re-join yarn at centre edge, K3, s2kpo, K to end.

Work 4 rows in st st.

Next row P across all sts.

Next row K7, s2kpo, K to last 10 sts, s2kpo, K to end.

Work 5 rows in st st.

Next row K6, s2kpo, K to last 9 sts, s2kpo, K to end. *16 sts.*

Work 5 rows in st st.

Cast off 1 st at beg of next 4 rows. *12 sts.*

Work 4 rows straight.

Next row Work 4, cast off 4 sts, work 4.

Work each shoulder separately by working 4 rows straight on each side.

Cast off.

TO MAKE UP

Block and press work.

Join side seams together.

Armhole edging (both alike)

Using 3mm (US 2/3) needles and CC, with RS facing beg and end at edge of the shoulder band, K into every st.

Cast off.

Front and back neck edges (both alike)

Using 3mm (US 2/3) needles and CC, with RS of work facing pick up and K14 sts around neck edge.

Cast off.

Make a loop at the top of each of the front shoulders.

Sew a button on each of the back shoulders.

Working in CC and using lazy daisy stitch (see page 123), work a group of flowers on the left shoulder and the lower left skirt. Place a French knot in the middle of each flower (see page 123).

BUNNY HEADBAND

Using 3.5mm (US 4) needles and CC, cast on 41 sts and work 2 rows in garter st.

Change to MC and work 6 rows in st st.

Change back to CC and work 2 rows in garter st.

Cast off.

With CC, pick up and K6 sts from one narrow end of the headband.

K 1 row.

Cast off.

Block and press work.

Place contrast edged end of the band over the other and sew into place with a button.

Embroider flowers on band as for child's headband.

Highgrove

Highgrove House near Tetbury, Gloucestershire is the home of the Prince of Wales and the Duchess of Cornwall. Prince Charles has for many years been a leading light in organic farming and ethically sound living. The Highgrove collection is knitted in pure new wool and echoes the trend for natural fibres. The cream and grey remind us of natural, undyed fleece and the use of garter stitch evokes thoughts of country textures.

SIZES

Up to 3(3–6:6–9:9–12) months

YARN

Rowan *Baby Merino Silk DK (double knitting) yarn* in Straw 671 and Dawn 672

NOTE:

If knitting more than one design the yarn quantities will be reduced for each item, for instance the booties take less than a quarter of a ball of each colour so could easily be knitted from leftovers.

Crossover Cardigan

You will need

YARN

Rowan *Baby Merino Silk DK*

2(3:3:3) x 50g/1¾oz balls in Straw 671 (MC)

1(1:1:1) x 50g/1¾oz ball in Dawn 672 (CC)

NEEDLES

Pair each of 3.5mm (US 4) and 4mm (US 6) knitting needles

EXTRAS

50cm/20in of narrow ribbon, for inside tie

Buttons: 3 for all sizes

TENSION

22 sts and 44 rows over garter st and 22 sts and 30 rows over st st to 10cm/4in square using 4mm (US 6) needles.

ABBREVIATIONS

See page 124.

SIZES

Up to 3(3–6:6–9:9–12) months

BACK

Using 4mm (US 6) needles, cast on 42(46:50:56) sts. Work straight in garter st until back measures 20(23:26:29)cm/8(9:10¼:11½)in. Cast off.

RIGHT FRONT

Using 4mm (US 6) needles, cast on 34(38:42:48) sts and work in garter st until front measures 7(8:9:10) cm/2¾(3:3½:4)in, ending on a WS row.

Next row Cast off 3 sts, work to end.

Next row K.

Next row Cast off 2 sts, K to end.

***Next row** K.

Next row K1, K2tog, K to end*.

Rep from * to * until 12(14:15:16) sts rem. Work straight until work measures 20(23:26:29)cm/8(9:10¼:11½)in.

Cast off.

LEFT FRONT

Work as for Right front, reversing shaping.

SLEEVES

Using 4mm (US 6) needles, cast on 28(30:32:34) sts. Cont in garter st, inc 1 st at each end on every 10ᵗʰ row until there are 34(38:42:46) sts.

Work straight until sleeve measures 12(15:18:21)cm/4¾(6:7:8¼)in.

Cast off.

POCKET (make 1)

Using 4mm (US 6) needles and MC, cast on 15(16:18:19) sts and K 3 rows.

Change to st st and beg with a K row, work 14(16:18:20) rows, ending with a WS row.

Change to CC and K 1 row.

Cast off.

TO MAKE UP

Block and press work.

Sew the shoulder seams.

Fold sleeves in half and place fold at the shoulder seam, then sew sleeves into place.

Sew side and sleeve seams.

Contrast edging

With RS facing and using 3.5mm (US 4) needles and CC, beg at the lower right edge and ending at the lower left edge, K into every st.

Cast off.

Buttonholes

Make 3 loops (either with a crochet hook and chain st or knitting 6 rows with 1 st only), evenly along the lower front edge, for buttonholes.

Sew buttons to correspond with the buttonholes.

Cut the ribbon in half and sew a piece each side of the under wrap to hold the lower front in position. Sew pocket in place.

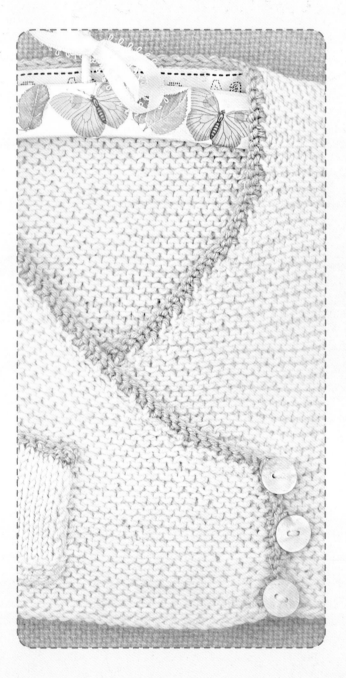

Sweater

NOTE The Sweater is worked as single piece,
beginning at the front.

SIZES
Up to 3(3–6:6–9:9–12) months

FRONT
Using 4mm (US 6) needles, cast on 48(52:58:64)
sts and work in garter st until front measures
11(14:17:19)cm/4¼(5½:6¾:7½)in.

Cast on for sleeves
Inc at each side on every alt row:
1st size Cast on 6 sts, three times, then 4 sts twice.
26 sts per sleeve.
2nd size Cast on 8 sts, three times, then 10 sts once.
34 sts per sleeve.
3rd size Cast on 8 sts, five times. *40 sts per sleeve*
4th size Cast on 10 sts, four times, then 6 sts once.
46 sts per sleeve.
Work straight on the 100(120:138:156) sts until
work measures 18(20.5:24:27)cm/7(8:9½:10½)in.

Next row K42(51:59:67), cast off 16(18:20:22) sts from the centre, cont on the rem 42(51:59:67) sts.
Work a further 2(2.5:3:3)cm/¾(1:1¼:1¼)in, ending at the neck edge.
Cast off 11 sts, K to end.
Next row K to end, cast on 11 sts.*
Slip all sts from this side onto a stitch holder.
Re-join yarn and work the second shoulder as the first shoulder to *, reversing shaping.
Next row Cast on 16(18:20:22) sts for the back neck and re-join the sts from the stitch holder.
Work straight on the 100(120:138:156) sts until work measures 29(32:37:41)cm/11½(12½:14½:16)in from the cast-on edge.
Next row Cast off to shape the sleeve on every alt row as foll:
1st size Cast off 4 sts twice, then cast off 6 sts, three times.
2nd size Cast off 10 sts once, then 8 sts, three times.
3rd size Cast off 8 sts, five times.
4th size Cast off 6 sts once, then cast off 10 sts, four times.
Cont on the rem 48(52:58:64) sts until the Back measures the same as the Front.
Cast off.

POCKETS (make 2)
Using 4mm (US 6) needles and MC, cast on 15(16:18:19) sts and K 3 rows.
Change to st st and beg with a K row, work 14(16:18:20) rows, ending with a WS row.
Change to CC and K 1 row.
Cast off.

TO MAKE UP
Block and press work.
Sew side and sleeve seams together.

Right back buttonhole band
With RS facing and using 3.5mm (US 4) needles and MC, beg at the sleeve end and pick up and K12 sts.
K 5 rows.

Buttonhole row [K1, yf, K2tog, K1] 3 times.
K 2 rows.
Cast off.

Left back buttonhole band
With RS facing and using 3.5mm (US 4) needles and MC, beg at at the neck end, pick up and K12 sts.
Work as for Right back buttonhole band.

Neck border
With RS facing and using 3.5mm (US 4) needles and CC, beg at the right sleeve edge of buttonhole band and K into every st across to the left sleeve edge.
Cast off.

Front neck edging
With RS facing and using 3.5mm (US 4) needles and CC, beg at the left side and K into every st across to the right side.
Cast off.
Sew buttons into place.
Sew pockets into place.

Pants

You will need

YARN

Rowan *Baby Merino Silk DK*
2(3:3:3) x 50g/1¾oz balls in Dawn 672 (MC)
1(1:1:1) x 50g/1¾oz ball in Straw 671 (CC),
for cord

NEEDLES

Pair each of 3mm (US 2/3) and 4mm (US 6)
knitting needles

TENSION

22 sts and 44 rows to 10cm/4in square over
garter st using 4mm (US 6) needles.

ABBREVIATIONS

See page 124.

SIZES

Up to 3(3–6:6–9:9–12) months

FRONT (work each leg separately)

Using 4mm (US 6) needles, cast on 26(28:30:32)
sts and work in garter st until leg measures
12(15:18:21)cm/4¾(6:7:8¼)in.
Work second leg the same.
Place both legs on the needle. *52(56:60:64) sts*
**Cont straight until work measures 24(27:32:38)
cm/9½(10½:12½:15)in.

Next row K21(23:25:27), cast off 2 sts, K6, cast off
2 sts, K21(23:25:27).
Next row K21(23:25:27), cast on 2 sts, K6, cast on
2 sts, K21(23:25:27)**.
Cont straight until work measures 26(31:36:42)cm/
10¼(12¼:14¼:16½)in.
Change to 3mm (US 2/3) needles and K1, P1 rib
for 6cm/2¼in.
Cast off.

BACK

Work as for Front omitting from ** to **.

TO MAKE UP

Block and press work.

Join side seam.

Join inside leg seam.

Fold ribbed top to the inside and slip stitch into place,
sew a row of running stitches along the top edge.

French knit or make an I-cord three times the width
of the waist.

Thread the cord though the casing, sew and fix cord
at the centre back.

Tie a knot in each end of the cord.

Hat

You will need

YARN
Rowan *Baby Merino Silk DK*
1(1:1:1) x 50g/1¾oz ball in Straw 671 (MC)
1(1:1:1) x 50g/1¾oz ball in Dawn 672 (CC)

NEEDLES
Pair of 4mm (US 6) knitting needles

TENSION
22 sts and 44 rows to 10cm/4in square over garter st using 4mm (US 6) needles.

ABBREVIATIONS
See page 124.

SIZES
Up to 3(3–6:6–9:9–12) months

HAT
Using 4mm (US 6) needles and CC, cast on 56(62:68:68) sts and work 4cm/1½in in st st, ending on a P row.
Change to MC and garter st and work straight until work measures 14(16:18:20)cm/5½(6¼:7:8)in, ending on a WS row.

Row 1 K1, *K2tog, K7(8:9:9)*, rep from * to * 6 times, K 1.
Work 3 rows.

Row 5 K1, *K2tog, K6(7:8:8)*, rep from * to * 6 times, K1.

Row 6 K.

Row 7 K1, *K2tog, K5(6:7:7)*, rep from * to * 6 times, K1.

Row 8 K.

Row 9 K1, *K2tog, K4(5:6:6)*, rep from * to * 6 times, K1.

Row 10 K.

Row 11 K1, *K2tog, K3(4:5:5)*, rep from * to * 6 times, K1.

Row 12 K.

2nd size only K1, *K2tog, K3*, rep from * to *
6 times, K1.

3rd and 4th sizes only K1, *K2tog, K4(4)*, rep from
* to * 6 times, K1.

Next row K.

3rd and 4th sizes only K1, *K2tog, K3(3)*, rep from
* to * 6 times, K1.

Next row K.

All sizes

Next row (RS) K1, *K2tog, rep from * to
last st, K1.

Next row K.

Next row (RS) K1, *K2tog, rep from * to
last st, K1.

Next row K.

Thread yarn through sts and fasten off.

TO MAKE UP

Block and press work.

Sew the back seam inverting the band seam.

Tag

Using 4mm (US 6) needles and CC, cast
on 15 sts.

Work 4 rows in st st.

Cast off.

Slip stitch the long edges together, fold tag over and
push the ends through the top point of the hat. Sew
into place on the inside.

Booties

SIZES

Up to 3(3–6:6–9:9–12) months

BOOTIES (make two)

Beg at the sole, using 4mm (US 6) needles and MC, cast on 27(31:35:39) sts.

Work 2 rows in garter st.

Inc on every alt row as foll:

1st row K1, M1 by picking up the loop between sts, K12(14:16:18), M1 as before, K1, M1, K12(14:16:18), M1, K1. *31(35:39:43) sts*

Next row K.

Next row K2, M1, K12(14:16:18), M1, K3, M1, K12(14:16:18), M1, K2. *35(39:43:47) sts*

K 1(3:5:7) row(s).

Next row K14(16:18:20), K2tog, K3, K2tog, K14(16:18:20).

Next row K.

Next row K14(16:18:20), K2tog, K1, K2tog, K14(16:18:20).

Next row K.

Next row K13(15:17:19), K2tog, K1, K2tog, K13(15:17:19).

Next row K.

Next row K12(14:16:18), K2tog, K1, K2tog, K12(14:16:18).

Cont to dec either side of centre toe st on every alt row until there are 21(23:25:27) sts on the needle.

Change to CC and K for 4(5:5:6)cm/1½(2:2:2¼)in.

Cast off.

TO MAKE UP

Block and press work.

Sew the sole seam together and cont as far as the contrast yarn.

Fold top over and sew a button on each side.

Bunny Sweater & Pants

Sweater

FINISHED SIZE
Length to shoulder approx. 10cm/4in

SWEATER
Using 3.5mm (US 4) needles and MC, cast on 26
sts and work 24 rows in garter st.
Cast on 5 sts at beg of next 4 rows.
Cast on 4 sts at beg of next 2 rows. *54 sts.*
Work 14 rows straight.

Next row K22, cast off 10 sts, K to end.
Work 6 rows on first set of 22 sts.
Next row K16, cast off 6 sts (neck edge).
Re-join yarn at neck edge on second set of 22 sts
and work 6 rows straight.
Next row Cast off 6 sts (neck edge), K to end.
Next row K16, cast on 22 sts, K16 from first set of
sts. *54 sts.*
Work 14 rows straight.

Cast off 4 sts at beg of next 2 rows.

Cast off 5 sts at beg of next 4 rows.

Work 24 rows straight.

Cast off.

BUTTON BANDS

Using 3mm (US 2/3) needles and MC, with the back of the Sweater and RS of work facing, beg at the right-hand side, pick up and K6 sts.

Work 6 rows in garter st.

Buttonhole row K1, [yf, K2tog] twice, K1.

K 1 row.

Cast off.

Work to match the second buttonhole band.

Back neck edging

Using 3mm (US 2/3) needles and CC, with the back of the Sweater and RS of work facing, beg at the right-hand side of the cast-off edge of the buttonhole band, K into every st.

Cast off.

Front neck edging

Using 3mm (US 2/3) needles and CC, with the front of the Sweater and RS of work facing, beg at the right-hand side of the button band, K into every st.

Cast off.

POCKETS (make 2)

Using 3mm (US 2/3) needles and MC, cast on 10 sts.

K 1 row.

Beg with a K row, work 8 rows in st st.

Change to CC and K 1 row.

Cast off.

TO MAKE UP

Block and press work.

Sew pockets into position.

Join sleeves and side seams.

Sew buttons into place.

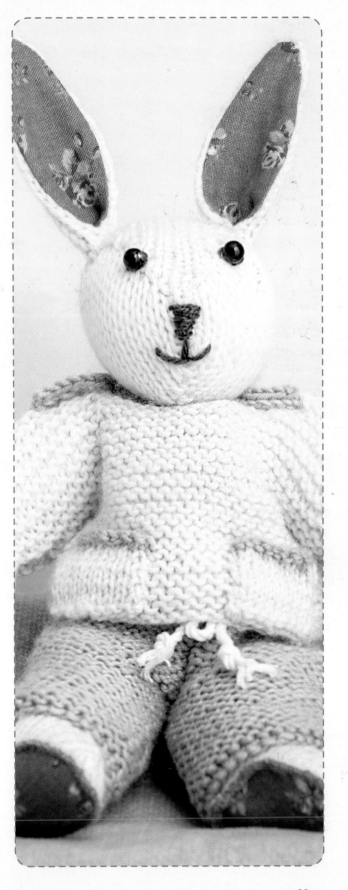

Pants

You will need

YARN
1 x 50g/1¾oz ball of Rowan *Baby Merino Silk DK* in Dawn 672

NEEDLES
Pair each of 3mm (US 2/3) and 3.5mm (US 4) knitting needles

EXTRAS
50cm/20in of narrow cord

TENSION
22 sts and 44 rows to 10cm/4in square over garter st using 3.5mm (US 4) needles.

ABBREVIATIONS
See page 124.

FINISHED SIZE
Approx. length 13cm/5in

PANTS (make two sides)
Using 3.5mm (US 4) needles, cast on 26 sts and work 30 rows straight.
Next row Inc into first 2 sts, K to last 3 sts, inc into next 2 sts, K1.
Work 23 rows straight.

Next row (for right leg) K4, yf, K2tog, K to end.
Next row (for left leg) K to last 6 sts, K2tog, yf, K4.
Work 3 rows straight.
Change to 3mm (US 2/3) needles and work 4 rows in K1, P1 rib.
Cast off in rib.

TO MAKE UP

Block and press work.

Join front seam.

Join back seam, leaving a gap for the tail.

Turn rib to the inside and slip stitch into place.

Sew a row of running stitches along the top edge.

Thread cord through the casing and tie in a bow, tie a knot in each end of the cord.

Sandringham

Sandringham House, once described as 'the most comfortable house in England' was bought for Edward, Prince of Wales, later King Edward V11 by his mother, Queen Victoria, in the 1860s. King George V called it 'the place he loved most in all the world' and it is the home that our Queen and the Royal family choose at which to spend every Christmas. Sandringham House is built of local carrstone, grey tile, and stone. The Sandringham collection is cuddly and warm with interesting stripes that mimic the ploughed fields of Norfolk and take up the colours of the house, with an added splash of gold to celebrate the yearly appearance of the wild golden asphodel which grows on the estate.

SIZES
Up to 3(3–6:6–9:9–12) months

YARN
Rowan *Baby Merino Silk DK (double knitting) yarn* in Snowdrop 670 and Dawn 672. Rowan *Kidsilk Haze mohair/silk blended yarn* in Ember 644

NOTE:
If knitting more than one design the yarn quantities will be reduced for each item, for instance the booties take less than a quarter of a ball of each colour so could easily be knitted from leftovers.

Cardigan

YARN

1(1:2:2) x 50g/1¾oz ball(s) of Rowan *Baby Merino Silk DK* in Snowdrop 670 (MC)

1(1:1:2) x 50g/1¾oz ball(s) of Rowan *Baby Merino Silk DK* in Dawn 672 (CC)

1(1:2:2) x 25g/⅞oz ball(s) of Rowan *Kidsilk Haze* in Ember 644

NEEDLES

Pair each of 3mm (US 2/3), 3.5mm (US 4) and 4mm (US 6) knitting needles

Stitch holder

EXTRAS

Buttons: 4 for all sizes

TENSION

22 sts and 30 rows to 10cm/4in square over st st using 4mm (US 6) needles.

ABBREVIATIONS

See page 124.

NOTE Use *Kidsilk Haze* double throughout.

SIZES

Up to 3(3–6:6–9:9–12) months

BACK

Using 4mm (US 6) needles and MC, cast on 46(50:58:62) sts and work 6 rows in garter st.

Beg with a K row, change to st st and work the first half of the row in MC, join in CC and work the second half in CC, twisting the yarns together at the join.

Work straight until back measures 11(14:15:18)cm/4¼(5½:6:7)in.

Change colours over to form a square of each colour, work straight until back measures 22(27:30:35)cm/8¾(10¾:11¾:13¾)in, ending with a WS row.

Shape shoulders

Cast off 8(9:10:11) sts at beg of next 2 rows, then 7(8:9:10) sts at beg of foll 2 rows.

Slip rem 16(16:20:20) sts onto a stitch holder.

LEFT FRONT

Using 4mm (US 6) needles and MC, cast on 20(22:26:28) sts and work 6 rows in garter st.

Change to CC and st st.

Work straight until front measures 11(14:15:18)cm/ 4¼(5½:6:7)in.

Change to MC.

Cont to work straight until front is 10(12:12:12) rows less than the back, ending on a WS row.

Shape neck

Work 1 row.

Next row Cast off 1(1:3:3) st(s) at neck edge.

Work 1 row.

Dec 1 st at neck edge on next and foll 3(3:3:3) alt rows. *15(17:19:21) sts.*

Work 0(2:2:2) rows straight, ending on a WS row.

Shape shoulder

Cast off 8(9:10:11) sts at beg of next row.

Work 1 row.

Cast off rem 7(8:9:10) sts.

Right front

Using 4mm (US 6) needles and MC, cast on 20(22:26:28) sts and work 6 rows in garter st.

Cont in MC and work straight until front measures 11(14:15:18)cm/4¼(5½:6:7)in.

Change to CC.

Cont to work straight until front is 10(12:12:12) rows less than the back, ending on a WS row.

Shape neck

Work as for Left neck, reversing shaping.

FIRST SLEEVE

Using 3.5mm (US 4) needles and MC, cast on 25(29:33:33) sts and work 6 rows in garter st.

Change to 4mm (US 6) needles and inc 1 st at each end of 5th(7th:9th:9th) row, then at each end of every 4th(7th:9th:9th) row, when sleeve measures 6(8:12:13)cm/ 2¼(3¼:4¾:5)in change to CC, cont to inc 1 st at each end of 4th(7th:9th:9th) row, until there are

39(39:47:51) sts.

Work 1(5:7:3) row(s).

Cast off loosely.

SECOND SLEEVE

Using 3.5mm (US 4) needles and MC, cast on 25(29:33:33) sts and work 6 rows in garter st.

Change to 4mm (US 6) needles and CC, inc 1 st at each end of 5th(7th:9th:9th) row, then at each end of every 4th(7th:9th:9th) row, when sleeve measures 6(8:12:13)cm/2¼(3¼:4¾:5)in change to MC, cont to inc 1 st at each end of 4th(7th:9th:9th) row until there are 39(39:47:51) sts.

Work 1(5:7:3) row(s).

Cast off loosely.

TO MAKE UP

Block and press work.

Sew the shoulder seams. Fold sleeves in half and place fold at shoulder seam, then sew sleeves into place.

Join side and sleeve seams.

Using duplicate stitch/Swiss darning (see page 76) and 2 strands of *Kidsilk Haze*, work 2 rows all around the body and the sleeve on the halfway lines.

Work 2 rows of *Kidsilk Haze* duplicate stitch up the centre back on the halfway line.

Front edges (both alike)

With RS side facing, using 3.5mm (US 4) needles and *Kidsilk Haze*, K into every st.

Next row K.

Cast off.

Buttonhole band

Using 3.5mm (US 4) needles and MC, cast on 7 sts.

Slipping the first st in every row, work 4 rows garter st.

***Buttonhole row** Sl1, K2, yf, K2tog, K2.

Work 8 rows *.

Rep from * to * 3 times more.

Work straight until the band, when slightly stretched, reaches from the top neck edge to the bottom edge. Cast off.

Button band

Work as for buttonhole band, omitting buttonholes. Sew the button and buttonhole bands into place, by sewing under the *Kidsilk Haze* edge.

Neck edge

Using 3mm (US 2/3) needles and 2 strands of *Kidsilk Haze*, with RS facing pick up and K7 sts from top of front right band 18(19:20:21) sts from right side of neck, K the 16(16:20:20) sts from back stitch holder, pick up and K18(19:20:21) sts from left side of neck, then K7 sts from top of front right band.
66(68:74:76) sts.
K 2 rows.
Cast off.

Sew buttons to correspond with buttonholes.

DUPLICATE STITCH

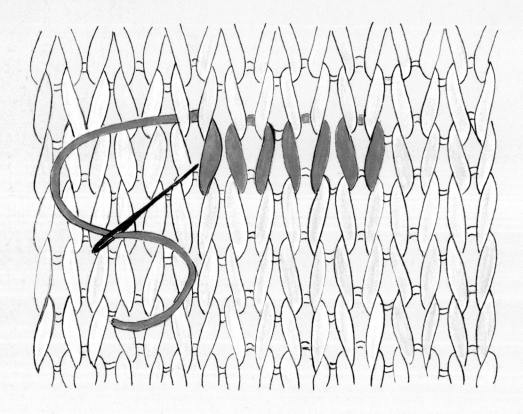

Overalls

You will need

YARN

1(1:1:1) x 50g/1¾oz ball of Rowan *Baby Merino Silk DK* in Snowdrop 670 (MC)

1(1:1:1) x 50g/1¾oz ball of Rowan *Baby Merino Silk DK* in Dawn 672

1(1:1:1) x 25g/⁷⁄₈oz ball of Rowan *Kidsilk Haze* in Ember 644

NEEDLES

Pair each of 3.5mm (US 4) and 4mm (US 6) knitting needles

Stitch holder

EXTRAS

Buttons: 12(13:14:15)

TENSION

22 sts and 30 rows to 10cm/4in square over st st using 4mm (US 6) needles.

ABBREVIATIONS

See page 124.

NOTE Use *Kidsilk Haze* double throughout. Work the garter st borders in MC and all st st in 3 colour x 2 row stripes, do not break off the yarn but carry up the side of the work.

SIZES

Up to 3(3–6:6–9:9–12) months

FRONT

Legs

Make 2, leaving the first leg on a stitch holder or spare needle until the second leg is completed.

Using 4mm (US 6) needles and MC, cast on 24(26:28:30) sts.

K 4 rows in garter st.

Change to st st and beg the stripes – 2 rows of each of the 3 colours.

Work straight until leg measures 10(13:16:19) cm/4(5¼:6¼:7½)in, ending on a WS row.
Work second leg the same.

Next row Work across the first lot of sts, inc 1 st then work across the sts from the holder. *49(53:57:61) sts*
Work 3 rows.

Next row K23(25:27:29), s2kpo, K23(25:27:29). *47(51:55:59) sts*

Next row P.

Next row K22(24:26:28), s2kpo, K22(24:26:28). *45(49:53:57) sts*

Next row P.

Next row K21(23:25:27), s2kpo, K21(23:25:27). *43(47:51:55) sts*

Next row P.

Cont in st st until work measures 26(31:36:41)cm/ 10¼(12¼:14¼:16¼)in.
Change to MC and cont in garter st for 3cm/1¼in**

Armhole shaping
Cast off 3 sts at beg of next 2 rows, then cast off 2 sts at beg of next 2 rows, dec 1 st at beg and end of next 1(2:2:3) row(s). *31(33:37:39) sts*
Cont straight until work measures 32.5(38:43.5:49) cm/12¾(15:17:19¼)in, ending on a WS row.

Shape for front neck
K9(9:10:10), cast off the centre 13(15:17:19) sts, K to end.
Work each side separately.
Work straight for 3(4:4.5:5)cm/1¼(1½:1¾:2)in.
Next row K2, yf, K2tog, K1(1:2:2), K2tog, yf, K2.
K 3 rows.
Cast off.

BACK
Work as for Front until **.

Armhole shaping
Cast off 3 sts at beg of next 2 rows, then cast off 2 sts at beg of next 2 rows, dec 1 st at beg and end of next 1(2:2:3) row(s). *31(33:37:39) sts*

Cont straight until work measures 37(43:49:55)cm/ 14½(17:19¼:21¾)in, ending on a WS row.

Shape for neck
K9(9:10:10), cast off the centre 13(15:17:19) sts, K to end.
Work each side separately.
Work 2cm/¾in straight.
Cast off.

FRONT LEG (BUTTONHOLE) BAND
With pieces of coloured yarn, evenly place 8(9:10:11) markers to indicate the positions of the buttons.
Using 3.5mm (US 4) needles and MC, cast on 7 sts.
Slipping the first st in every row, work in garter st until the band, slightly stretched, is the same length as the inside legs and gusset, working a buttonhole to correspond with each button marker, then cast off.
Buttonhole row Sl1, K2, yf, K2tog, K2.

Back inside leg edge
Using 4mm (US 6) needles and MC, with RS facing, K into every st.
Cast off.

TO MAKE UP
Block and press work.
Sew the side seams.
Sew front leg band into place.
Sew buttons to correspond with the buttonholes.

Sweater

NOTE Use *Kidsilk Haze* double throughout.
Knit all bands in MC, then knit 3 colour x 2 row stripes up to raglan on all pieces, then MC only from raglan to neck edge.

SIZES

Up to 3(3–6:6–9:9–12) months

FRONT

Using 4mm (US 6) needles and MC, cast on 49(55:61:67) sts and work 6 rows in garter st.
Change to 3 colour x 2 row stripes and work in st st, do not break off the yarn but carry along at the edge of the work.
Work straight until front measures 16(17:18:19)cm/6¼(6¾:7:7½)in, ending on a WS row.
Change to MC, break off yarns not required.
Cast off 3 sts at beg of next 2 rows.

Row 1 K1, K2tog tbl, K to last 3 sts, K2tog, K1.
Row 2 P.
Row 3 K.
Row 4 P.
Work Rows 1 to 4 twice more, then rep Rows 1 and 2 until 29(31:33:35) sts rem, ending on a RS row.

Shape neck
Next row P17(19:21:23), slip the last 5(7:9:11) sts onto a stitch holder, P to end.
Cont on the last set of sts as foll:
Next row K1, K2tog tbl, work to last 2 sts, K2tog.
Next row P2tog, P to end.
Next row K1, K2tog tbl, work to last 2 sts, K2tog.
Next row P.
Next row K1, K2tog tbl, work to last 2 sts, K2tog.
Next row P2, P2tog tbl, P to end.
Next row K1, K2tog tbl, K1.
Next row P2tog tbl, P1.
Next row K2tog.
Fasten off.
Re-join yarn at neck edge.
Next row K2tog, work to last 3 sts, K2tog, K1.
Next row P to last 2 sts, P2tog.
Next row K2tog, K to last 3 sts, K2tog, K1.
Next row P.
Next row K2tog, work to last 3 sts, K2tog, K1.
Next row P1, P2tog, P2.
Next row K1, K2tog, K1.
Next row P1, P2tog.
Next row K2tog.
Fasten off.

BACK
Using 4mm (US 6) needles and MC, cast on 49(55:61:67) sts and work 6 rows in garter st.
Change to 3 colour x 2 row stripes, do not break off the yarn but carry along at the edge of the work.
Work straight until back measures 16(17:18:19)cm/ 6¼(6¾:7:7½)in, ending on a WS row.

Change to MC, break off yarns not required.
Cast off 3 sts at beg of next 2 rows.

Row 1 K1, K2tog tbl, K to last 3 sts, K2tog, K1.
Row 2 P.
Row 3 K.
Row 4 P.
Work Rows 1 to 4 twice more and then rep Rows 1 and 2 until 25(27:29:31) sts rem, ending on a WS row.
Next row K1, K2tog tbl, K to last 3 sts, K2tog, K1.
Next row P1, P2tog, P to last 3 sts, P2tog tbl, P1.
Rep the last 2 rows once more. *17(19:21:23) sts*
Place sts onto a stitch holder.

SLEEVES (both alike)
Using 4mm (US 6) needles and MC, cast on 29(31:33:35) sts and work 4 rows in garter st.
Change to 3 colour x 2 rows stripes, do not break off the yarn but carry along at the edge of the work.
Inc 1 st at each end of the 5th row and every foll 6th row until there are 37(39:41:45) sts, cont straight until the sleeve measures approximately 13.5(15:16.5:21.5)cm/5½(6:6½:8½)in, ending on a WS row and same stripe row as back.

Shape raglan
Break off the 2 contrast yarns and cont in MC only.
Cast off 3 sts at beg of next 2 rows.
Next row K1, K2tog tbl, K to last 3 sts, K2tog, K1.
Next row P.
Next row K.
Next row P.
Rep last 4 rows 1(2:3:3) time(s) more. *27(27:27:31) sts*
Next row K1, K2tog tbl, K to last 3 sts, K2tog, K1.
Next row P.
Rep last 2 rows until 7 sts rem, ending on a WS row.
Slip sts onto a stitch holder.

TO MAKE UP

Block and press work.

Join all the raglans with the exception of the left front raglan.

Join side and sleeve seams.

Neck band

With RS facing and using 3.5mm (US 4) needles and MC, pick up and K8(9:10:11) sts from left front neck, K5(7:9:11) sts from front neck, pick up and K8(9:10:11) sts from right front neck, 7 sts from right sleeve, 17(19:21:23) sts from back and 7 sts from left sleeve. *52(58:64:70) sts*

K 1 row.

Change to 3mm (US 2/3) needles and K 5 rows.

Cast off.

Join left front raglan to the point where the stripes end.

Buttonhole band

With RS of the Sweater front facing and using 3.5mm (US 4) needles and MC, beg at the first stripe and ending at the top edge of the neckband, pick up and K27(29:31:33) sts.

K 2 rows.

Next row K2, *yf, K2tog, K3*, rep from * to * 4(4:4:5) times more, K0(2:4:1).

Cast off.

Slip stitch lower end of buttonhole band over raglan.

Sew buttons to correspond with buttonholes.

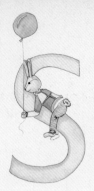

Hat

You will need

YARN

1(1:1:1) x 50g/1¾oz ball of Rowan *Baby Merino Silk DK* in Snowdrop 670 (MC)

1(1:1:1) x 50g/1¾oz ball of Rowan *Baby Merino Silk DK* in Dawn 672

1(1:1:1) x 25g/⁷⁄₈oz ball of Rowan *Kidsilk Haze* in Ember 644

NEEDLES

Pair of 3.5mm (US 4) knitting needles
Stitch holder

TENSION

22 sts and 30 rows to 10cm/4in square over st st using 3.5mm (US 4) needles.

ABBREVIATIONS

See page 124.

NOTE Use *Kidsilk Haze* double throughout. Work the garter st borders in MC and all st st in 3 colour x 2 row stripes, do not break off the yarn but carry up the side of the work.

SIZES

Up to 3(3–6:6–9:9–12) months

BACK AND FRONT (both alike)

Using 3.5mm (US 4) needles and MC, cast on 37(40:42:45) sts.

Work 8(8:9:9)cm/3¼(3¼:3½:3½)in in garter st, ending on a WS row.

Work in st st and 3 colour x 2 row stripes until hat measures 19(22:24:24)cm/7½(8¾:9½:9½)in, ending on a WS row.

Next row Keeping the stripes correct, K10, turn, leave rem 27(30:32:35) sts on a stitch holder. Work on the 10 sts.

Beg with a P row, cont in st st for a further 10cm/4in, ending on a WS row.

Dec 1 st at each end of every row until 2 sts rem. K2tog and fasten off.

With RS facing, re-join yarn to rem 27(30:32:35) sts, cast off 17(20:22:25) sts and K to end. *10 sts*

Beg with a P row, cont in st st for a further 10cm/4in, ending on a WS row.

Dec 1 st at each end of every row until 2 sts rem. K2tog and fasten off.

TO MAKE UP

Block and press work.

Join side and top seams, reversing the sewing on the garter st band.

Tie knot in each corner of the hat.

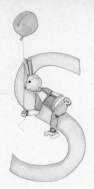

Booties

YARN

1(1:1:1) x 50g/1¾oz ball of Rowan *Baby Merino Silk DK* in Snowdrop 670 (MC)

1(1:1:1) x 50g/1¾oz ball of Rowan *Baby Merino Silk DK* in Dawn 672 (CC)

1(1:1:1) x 25g/⁷⁄₈oz ball of Rowan *Kidsilk Haze* in Ember 644

NEEDLES

Pair each of 3.5mm (US 4) and 4mm (US 6) knitting needles
Stitch holder

TENSION

22 sts and 38 rows to 10cm/4in square over garter st using 4mm (US 6) needles.

ABBREVIATIONS

See page 124.

SIZES

Up to 3(3–6:6–9:9–12) months

BOOTIES (make two)

Beg at the sole, using 4mm (US 6) needles and MC, cast on 27(31:35:39) sts.
Work 2 rows in garter st.

Inc on every alt row as foll:

1ˢᵗ row K1, M1 by picking up the loop between sts, K12(14:16:18), M1 as before, K1, M1, K12(14:16:18), M1, K1. *31(35:39:43) sts*

Next row K.

Next row K2, M1, K12(14:16:18), M1, K3, M1, K12(14:16:18), M1, K2. *35(39:43:47) sts*

K 1(3:5:7) row(s).

Next row K14(16:18:20), K2tog, K3, K2tog,
K14(16:18:20).
Next row K.
Next row K14(16:18:20), K2tog, K1, K2tog,
K14(16:18:20).
Next row K.
Next row K13(15:17:19), K2tog, K1, K2tog,
K13(15:17:19).
Next row K.
Next row K12(14:16:18), K2tog, K1, K2tog,
K12(14:16:18).
Cont to dec either side of centre toe st on every alt
row until there are 21(23:25:27) sts on the needle.
Change to CC and K for 4(5:5:6)cm/1½(2:2:2¼)in.
Cast off.

BOOTIES BORDERS

Using 3.5mm (US 4) needles and 2 strands of *Kidsilk
Haze*, with WS facing K into every st.
Work 2 rows.
Cast off.
Sew from the toe to halfway up the contrast
colour band.
Using 4mm (US 6) needles and 2 strands of *Kidsilk
Haze*, with WS facing and beg at the edge of the top
border, K into every st to the edge of the other border.
Work 2 rows.
Cast off.
Turn the top of the booties over.

87

Bunny Overalls

You will need

YARN

20g/¾oz of Rowan *Baby Merino Silk DK* in Snowdrop 670 (MC)
Small amount of Rowan *Baby Merino Silk DK* in Dawn 672 and Rowan *Kidsilk Haze* in Ember 644

NEEDLES

Pair of 3.5mm (US 4) knitting needles

EXTRAS

Buttons: 8 small

TENSION

22 sts and 34 rows to 10cm/4in square over st st using 3.5mm (US 4) needles.

ABBREVIATIONS

See page 124.

NOTE Use *Kidsilk Haze* double throughout.
Work the garter st borders in MC and all st st in 3 colour x 2 row stripes, do not break off the yarn but carry up the side of the work.

FINISHED SIZE

Length approx. 17cm/6¾in to shoulder

LEGS (make 2)

Using 3.5mm (US 4) needles and MC, using the thumb method cast on 32 sts leaving a very long end (this will be used to knit the second band).
K 3 rows.
Next row K3 in MC, beg and cont 2 rows of each of the 3 colours as in the child's overalls and K to last 3 sts, K3 in MC.

Next row K3 in MC, P to last 3 sts, K3 in MC.

Keeping the stripes correct, rep the last 2 rows 9 times. (18 rows)

Next row Cast off the 3 main border sts, K to last 3 sts, cast off these 3 border sts.

BODY

Slip first leg onto needle, slip second leg onto needle.

Next row P26, inc in last st, P26. *53 sts*

Next row (RS) K25, s2kpo, K to end. *51 sts*

Next row P.

Next row (RS) K24, s2kpo, K to end. *49 sts*

Next row P.

Next row (RS) K23, s2kpo, K to end. *47 sts*

Next row P.

Next row (RS) K22, s2kpo, K to end. *45 sts*

Next row P.

Next row (RS) K21, s2kpo, K to end. *43 sts*

Next row P.

Work 6 rows in st st stripes.

Next row (RS) Change to MC and garter st, K 7 rows in garter st.

Next row K10, cast off 2 sts, K18, cast off 2 sts, K9.

Work on the last 10 sts first.

Next row K8, K2tog.

Next row K.

Next row K7, K2tog.

K 7 rows straight.

Cast off 4 sts from back edge. *4 sts*

Work 6 rows.

Cast off.

Slip centre 19 sts onto a stitch holder.

Re-join yarn and work the rem 10 sts as for the first shoulder, reversing the shaping.

Slip the central sts back onto the needle.

Next row (RS) Re-join yarn, K2tog, K to last 2 sts, K2tog.

Next row K.

Rep last 2 rows twice. *13 sts*

Next row K4, cast off 5 sts, K3.

Work each shoulder separately.

First shoulder

K 1 row.

Buttonhole row K2, yf, K2. *5 sts*

Next row K.

Cast off.

Work second shoulder as first.

TO MAKE UP

Block and press work.

Join back seam, leaving an opening for the tail.

Overlap the back leg border with the front leg border, space the 8 buttons evenly and sew into place.

Sew a button to the back shoulder straps.

Windsor

Windsor Castle is the official residence of the Queen and the largest occupied castle in the world. It has been a royal home and fortress for over 900 years. It is here that the Queen spends her weekends; she takes up official residence over Easter and for a week in June for the service of the Order of the Garter. The Windsor collection was inspired by this amazing castle and the Order of the Garter: the twisted cable on the sweater symbolises eternal chivalry and the smart royal blue cardigan speaks of sobriety and honour.

SIZES
Up to 3(3–6:6–9:9–12) months

YARN
Rowan *Pure Wool DK (double knitting) yarn* in Cloud 058, Enamel 013 and Indigo 010

NOTE
If knitting more than one design the yarn quantities will be reduced for each item, for instance the booties take less than a quarter of a ball of each colour so could easily be knitted from leftovers.

All-in-one

SIZES
Up to 3(3–6:6–9:9–12) months

BACK (work each leg separately)
Using 4mm (US 6) needles and A, cast on
22(24:26:28) sts.
K 1 row.
Break off yarn and join in B.
K 2 rows.
Change to MC.
Working in st st, work straight until leg measures
13(15:19:23)cm/5(6:7½:9)in, slip sts onto a stitch
holder and work the second leg.
Place both sets of sts on the needle.
*44(48:52:56) sts***

Work straight until back measures 32(35:40:46)cm/
12½(13¾:15¾:18)in, ending on a WS row.

Armhole shaping
Cast off 3(3:4:4) sts at beg of next 2 rows.
38(42:44:48) sts.

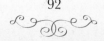

Work straight until back measures 40(44:50:57)cm/
15¾(17¼:19¾:22½)in.
Cast off.

FRONT
Work as for Back to **.
Work straight until front measures 26(29:33:38)cm/
10¼(11½:13:15)in, ending on a WS row.

Divide for front opening
Work 19(21:23:25) sts, cast off 6 sts and work each set
of 19(21:23:25) sts separately.

First shoulder
Work straight until front measures 32(35:40:46)cm/
12½(13¾:15¾:18)in.
Next row Cast off 3(3:4:4) sts at armhole edge.
Work straight until front measures 33(37:42:49)cm/
13(14½:16½:19¼)in.

Shape neck
Next row Cast off 3 sts at neck edge.
Work 1 row.
Next row Cast off 2 sts at neck edge.
Work 1 row.
Next row Cast off 1(1:2:2) st(s) at neck edge.
Work 3 rows.
Next row Cast off 1(1:1:2) st(s) at neck edge.
9(11:11:12) sts
Work straight until front measures 40(44:50:57)cm/
15¾(17¼:19¾:22½)in.
Cast off.
Work the second shoulder as the first,
reversing shaping.

SLEEVES
Using 4mm (US 6) needles and A, cast on
28(30:32:34) sts.
K 1 row.
Break off yarn and join in B.
K 2 rows.

Change to MC and work in st st, inc 1 st each side
every 8 rows until there are 34(38:42:46) sts.
Work straight until sleeve measures 14(17.5:21:24)cm/
5½(7:8¼:9½)in.
Cast off.

POCKET
Using 4mm (US 6) needles and A, cast on
14(14:16:16) sts.
Work 20(20:24:24) rows in garter st.
Cast off.

TO MAKE UP
Block and press work.
Join the right shoulder seam.

Neck edging
With RS facing, using 3.5mm (US 4) needles and B,
beg at the left shoulder, K into every st all around the
front and neck edge.
Cast off.
Join the left shoulder seam.
Fold the sleeve in half, place the fold against the
shoulder seam and sew into position, sewing final rows
to cast off sts at underarm.
Join the side and sleeve seams.

Back and front leg edges (both alike)
With RS facing, using 3.5mm (US 4) needles and B,
K into every st.
Cast off.

Front leg buttonhole band (make one in A)
With pieces of coloured yarn, evenly place 10 markers
to indicate the positions of the buttons.

Using 3.5mm (US 4) needles, cast on 7 sts.
Slipping the first st in every row, work in garter st until
the band, slightly stretched, is the same length as the
inside legs and gusset, working a buttonhole to
correspond with each button marker. Cast off.

Buttonhole row Sl1, K2, yf, K2tog, K2.

Sew the buttonhole band to the front leg edges under the contrast edge.

Front opening
Buttonhole band

Cast on 7 sts in A.

Work 6 rows in garter st, slipping the first st in every row.

Buttonhole row Sl1, K2, yf, K2tog, K2.

Cont in garter st, making 2 more buttonholes every 10th row until the band is the same length as the neck opening, ending on a WS row. Leave these sts on a stitch holder.

Button band

Work as for buttonhole band, omitting the buttonholes. Sew the bands into the neck opening with the button band below the buttonhole band.

Neck band

With RS facing, using 3.5mm (US 4) needles and A, K the 7 sts from the front band, then pick up and K 62(62:66:72) sts evenly from around the neck, picking up the sts from just below the contrast edge, then K the second 7 sts from the button band.

Work 4 rows in garter st.

Cast off.

Sew buttons to correspond with the buttonholes.

Sew on pocket and secure top edge with a button.

Cabled Sweater

You will need

YARN
2(2:2:3) x 50g/1¾oz balls of Rowan *Pure Wool DK* in Enamel 013

NEEDLES
Pair each of 3.5mm (US 4) and 4mm (US 6) knitting needles
Cable needle

EXTRAS
Buttons: 6 for all sizes

TENSION
20 sts and 28 rows to 10cm/4in square over st st using 4mm (US 6) needles.

ABBREVIATIONS
C2L – place next 2 sts on a cable needle at the front of the work, P2, then K2 from the cable needle.C2R – place next 2 sts on a cable needle at the back of the work, K2, then P2 from the cable needle.C4F – place next 2 sts on a cable needle at the front of the work, K2, then K2 from the cable needle.C4B – place next 2 sts on a cable needle at the back of the work, K2, then K2 from the cable needle.
See also page 124.

SIZES
Up to 3(3–6:6–9:9–12) months

BACK
Using 4mm (US 6) needles, cast on 44(48:52:58) sts, work 6 rows in garter st.

Change to st st and work straight until back measures 11(13:15:17)cm/4¼(5:6:6¾)in, ending on a WS row.
Work 4 rows in garter st**.
Change to st st and work straight until back measures 21(24:27:30)cm/8¼(9½:10½:11¾)in.
Cast off, marking centre 26(30:34:40) sts.

FRONT

Work as for Back to **.

Cable panel

Row 1 (RS) K12(14:16:19), P2, K2, P4, C4F, P4, K2, P2, K12(14:16:19).

Keeping the st st panels each side, cont with the cable panel as foll:

Row 2 K2, P2, K4, P4, K4, P2, K2.

Row 3 P2, C2L, C2R, C2L, C2R, P2.

Row 4 K4, P4, K4, P4, K4.

Row 5 P4, C4B, P4, C4F, P4.

Row 6 K4, P4, K4, P4, K4.

Row 7 P2, C2R, C2L, C2R, C2L, P2.

Row 8 K2, P2, K4, P4, K4, P2, K2.

Row 9 P2, K2, P4, C4F, P4, K2, P2.

Row 10 K2, P2, K4, P4, K4, P2, K2.

Row 11 P2, C2L, C2R, C2L, C2R, P2.

Row 12 K4, P4, K4, P4, K4.

Row 13 P4, C4F, P4, C4B, P4.

Row 14 K4, P4, K4, P4, K4.

Row 15 P2, C2R, C2L, C2R, C2L, P2.

Row 16 K2, P2, K4, P4, K4, P2, K2.

Work these 16 rows until front measures 16.5(19:21.5:24)cm/6½(7½:8½:9½)in, ending on a WS row.

Next row Work 18(19:21:23) sts, cast off centre 8(10:10:12) sts, then work each shoulder separately.

Next row Keeping the centre pattern correct, dec 1 st at the neck side on every alt row until there are 14(15:16:18) sts.

Work straight until front measures 21(24:27:30)cm/8¼(9½:10½:11¾)in.

Cast off 5(6:7:8) sts at sleeve edge.

Next row K1, yf, K2tog, K1, yf, K2tog, yf, K2tog, K1.

K 2 rows.

Cast off.

Re-join yarn and work the second shoulder as for the first.

NECK BANDS

Back neck

Using 3.5mm (US 4) needles and with RS facing, pick up and K26(29:32:35) sts evenly all along top back edge between markers.

K 2 rows.

Cast off.

Front neck

Using 3.5mm (US 4) needles and with RS facing, beg at the corner of the buttonhole band, pick up and K26(29:32:35) sts evenly around the front neck.

Work 2 rows in garter st.

Cast off.

SLEEVES

Using 3.5mm (US 4) needles, cast on 32(34:36:38) sts and work 6 rows in garter st.

Change to 4mm (US 6) needles and st st, inc 1 st at each end on every 5th(5th:6th:6th) row until there are 42(46:50:54) sts.

Work straight until sleeve measures 12(16:19:22)cm/4¾(6¾:7½:8¾)in.

Work 8 rows in garter st.

Cast off.

TO MAKE UP

Block and press work.

Join shoulder seams up to buttonhole bands.

Fold sleeve in half and place the fold against the shoulder seam, sew the sleeves in place.

Sew side and sleeve seams.

Sew buttons to correspond with the buttonholes.

Cardigan

You will need

YARN

2(2:3:3) x 50g/1¾oz balls of Rowan *Pure Wool DK* in Cloud 058

NEEDLES

Pair each of 3.5mm (US 4) and 4mm (US 6) knitting needles

EXTRAS

Buttons: 4(5:5:6)

TENSION

22 sts and 44 rows to 10cm/4in square over garter st using 4mm (US 6) needles.

ABBREVIATIONS

See page 124.

NOTE

Pattern is worked in garter st throughout.

SIZES

Up to 3(3–6:6–9:9–12) months

BACK

Using 4mm (US 6) needles, cast on 42(46:50:56) sts. Work straight in garter st until back measures 11(13:15:17)cm/4¼(5:6:6¾)in.

Dec 1 st at each end of next row.
Work straight in garter st until back measures 20(23:26:29)cm/8(9:10¼:11½)in.
Cast off.

RIGHT FRONT

Using 4mm (US 6) needles, cast on 23(25:27:30) sts. Work straight in garter st until front measures 11(13:15:17)cm/4¼(5:6:6¾)in, ending with a WS row.
Next row Dec 1 st at armhole edge.
Next row *(front edge) K2, K2tog tbl, K to end*.
Work 3 rows.
Next row Rep from * to *.
Rep the last 4 rows until there are 15(16:17:19) sts.

Work straight until front measures 20(23:26:29)cm/
8(9:10¼:11½)in.
Cast off.

LEFT FRONT

Work as for Right front, reversing shaping and making
a buttonhole at the front edge as foll:
[K2, K2tog, yf, K] to end. Make the first buttonhole
2cm/¾in from the bottom edge and then 2(3:3:4)
more every 11 rows up to the neck shaping, at this
point substitute K2tog tbl for K2tog.

SLEEVES (make 2)

Using 4mm (US 6) needles, cast on 28(30:32:34) sts.
Inc 1 st at each end on every 10th row until there are
34(38:42:46) sts.
Work straight until sleeve measures 12(15:18:21)cm/
4¾(6:7:8¼)in.
Cast off.

POCKET

Using 4mm (US 6) needles, cast on 14(14:16:16) sts.
Work 14(14:16:16) rows in st st.
Cast off.

TO MAKE UP

Block and press work.
Join shoulder seams
Fold sleeves in half and place fold on the
shoulder seam.
Sew sleeve in place.
Join the side and the sleeve seam.
Sew pocket into place with a button to secure top.
Sew buttons to correspond with the buttonholes.

Hat

You will need

YARN

Rowan *Pure Wool DK*
1(1:1:1) x 50g/1¾oz ball in Enamel 013 (MC)
Small amount in Cloud 058 (CC)

NEEDLES

Pair of 4mm (US 6) knitting needles

EXTRAS

Buttons: 1 for all sizes

TENSION

22 sts and 44 rows to 10cm/4in square over
garter st using 4mm (US 6) needles.

ABBREVIATIONS

See page 124.

SIZES

Up to 3(3–6:6–9:9–12) months

HAT

Using 4mm (US 6) needles and MC, cast on
56(62:68:68) sts and work straight in garter st until
work measures 14(16:18:20)cm/5½(6¼:7:8)in,
ending on a WS row.

Row 1 K1, *K2tog, K7(8:9:9)*, rep from * to * 6
times, K1.
Work 3 rows.

Row 5 K1, *K2tog, K6(7:8:8)*, rep from * to *
6 times, K1.
Row 6 K.
Row 7 K1, *K2tog, K5(6:7:7)*, rep from * to *
6 times, K1.
Row 8 K.
Row 9 K1, *K2tog, K4(5:6:6)*, rep from * to *
6 times, K1.
Row 10 K.
Row 11 K1, *K2tog, K3(4:5:5)*, rep from * to *
6 times, K1.

Row 12 K.

2nd size only

K1, *K2tog, K3*, rep from * to * 6 times, K1.

K 1 row.

3rd and 4th sizes only

K1, *K2tog, K4(4)*, rep from * to * 6 times, K1.

Next row K.

3rd and 4th sizes only

K1, *K2tog, K3(3)*, rep from * to * 6 times, K1.

Next row K.

All sizes

Next row (RS) K1, *K2tog, rep from * to last st, K1.

Next row K.

Next row (RS) K1, *K2tog, rep from * to last st, K1.

Next row K.

Thread yarn through sts and fasten off.

HAT TAG

Using 4mm (US 6) needles and CC, cast on 3 sts and K 1 row.

Next row Inc 1 st into first st, K to last 2 sts, inc into first st, K1.

Rep this row 2 times more. *9 sts*

Next and every foll row Sl1, K to end.

Rep this row for 18(22:26:30) rows more.

Next row and foll 2 rows K2tog, K to last 2 sts, K2tog. *3 sts*

Cast off.

TO MAKE UP

Block and press work.

Sew back seam, inverting seam at the turn up edge.

Sew tag into place and add a button.

Booties

SIZES

Up to 3(3–6:6–9:9–12) months

BOOTIES (make two)

Beg at the sole, using 4mm (US 6) needles and MC, cast on 27(31:35:39) sts.

Work 2 rows in garter st.

Inc on every alt row as foll:

1ˢᵗ row K1, M1 by picking up the loop between sts, K12(14:16:18), M1 as before, K1, M1,

K12(14:16:18), M1, K1. *31(35:39:43) sts*

Next row K.

Next row K2, M1, K12(14:16:18), M1, K3, M1, K12(14:16:18), M1, K2. *35(39:43:47) sts*

K 1(3:5:7) row(s).

Next row K14(16:18:20), K2tog, K3, K2tog, K14(16:18:20).

Next row K.

Next row K14(16:18:20), K2tog, K1, K2tog, K14(16:18:20).

Next row K.

Next row K13(15:17:19), K2tog, K1, K2tog, K13(15:1719).

Next row K.

Next row K12(14:16:18), K2tog, K1, K2tog, K12(14:16:18).

Cont to dec either side of centre toe st until there are 21(23:25:27) sts on the needle.

Change to CC and K 2 rows.

Next row K10(11:12:13), K twice into next st, K to end.

K 8(10:12:14) rows on the first group of 11(12:13:14) sts.

Cast off these sts.

Work 8(10:12:14) rows on the second group of 11(12:13:14) sts.

Cast off.

TO MAKE UP

Block and press work.

Join the sole and back seam.

Fold cuffs over.

Sew button between the cuffs.

Bunny All-in-one

You will need

YARN
Rowan *Pure Wool DK*
1 x 50g/1¾oz ball in Cloud 058 (MC)
Scrap of Enamel 013 (A)
Scrap of Indigo 010 (B)

NEEDLES
Pair of 3.5mm (US 4) knitting needles
3.5mm (US 4) double-pointed needle
Stitch holder

EXTRAS
Buttons: 13 small

TENSION
22 sts and 34 rows to 10cm/4in square over st st
using 3.5mm (US 4) needles.

ABBREVIATIONS
See page 124.

FINISHED SIZE
Length approx. 19cm/7½in to shoulder

LEGS (make 2)
Using 3.5mm (US 4) needles and A, using the
thumb method cast on 32 sts, leaving a very long
end (this will be used to knit the second band).
K 1 row.

Join in B.
Next row K3 in A, K to last 3 sts in B, K3 in A.
Next row K3 in A, K to last 3 sts in B, K3 in A,
break off B.
Cont as foll:
Row 1 K3 in A, K to last 3 sts in MC, K3 in A.
Row 2 K3 in A, P to last 3 sts in MC, K3 in A.
Rep last 2 rows 9 times.

Next row Cast off the 3 contrast sts, K to last 3 sts in MC, cast off the 3 contrast sts.

Join legs for body

Slip first leg onto needle then slip second leg onto needle.

Next row P26, inc in last st, P26. *53 sts*

Next row (RS) K25, s2kpo, K to end. *51 sts*

Next row P.

Next row (RS) K24, s2kpo, K to end. *49 sts*

Next row P.

Next row (RS) K23, s2kpo, K to end. *47 sts*

Next row P.

Next row (RS) K22, s2kpo, K to end. *45 sts*

Next row P.

Next row (RS) K21, s2kpo, K to end. *43 sts*

Next row P.

Work 11 rows in st st, ending with a WS row.

Divide for armholes

Next row K9, cast off 2 sts, K19, cast off 2 sts, K9, cut yarn.

Next row Slip the first 10 sts onto a double-pointed needle, slip the middle 20 sts onto a stitch holder, using regular needle, P the second 9 sts then P the 10 sts from the double-pointed needle.

Next row K, these 19 sts form the back of the all-in-one.

Next row P.

Next row K2tog, K to last 2 sts, K2tog.

Rep the last 2 rows once.

Work 10 rows in st st.

Cast off.

FRONT

With WS facing, slip the last 9 sts from the stitch holder, re-join yarn.

Next row P.

Next row K2tog (armhole edge), K to end.

Rep the last 2 rows once.

Work 4 rows in st st.

Cast off 4 sts at neck edge.

Work 7 rows in st st.

Cast off.

With WS facing, slip rem 11 sts from stitch holder, re-join yarn.

Next row P.

Next row Cast off the first 2 sts, then work the second side as the first, reversing all shaping.

SLEEVES

Using A, cast on 25 sts.

K 1 row.

Join in B, K 2 rows.

Break off contrast yarns and join in MC.

Work 10 rows in st st.

Next row Dec 1 st at each end.

Next row P.

Rep last 2 rows until 13 sts rem, ending on a RS row.

Next row P2tog, P to last 2 sts, P2tog.

Next row K2tog, K to last 2 sts, K2tog.

Next row P2tog to last 2 sts, P2tog.

Cast off.

POCKET

Using 3.5mm (US 4) needles and A, cast on 10 sts.

Work 13 rows in garter st.

Cast off.

TO MAKE UP

Block and press work.

Front edging

With RS facing and B, pick up and K9 sts from left neck, 8 sts from left front opening, 3 sts from centre front, 8 sts from right opening and 9 sts from right front neck.

Next row Cast off 9 sts, K7, cast off 3 sts, K7, cast off 9 sts.

Buttonhole band (left front)

Break off B and join in A, work 1 row on first 8 sts.

Next row K1, [yf, K2tog] 3 times, K1.

K 1 row.

Cast off.

Button band

Work as for buttonhole band, omitting buttonholes on second 8 sts.

Join the shoulder seams.

Back edging

With RS facing and B, beg at the right shoulder seam, pick up and K5 sts along the back neck edge.

K 1 row.

Cast off.

Neck band

With RS facing and A, beg at the front opening of the right front band and ending at the front opening of the left front band, pick up and K40 sts.

K 1 row.

Cast off.

Join sleeve seams and sew sleeves into place.

Join back seam above and below opening for the tail.

Overlap the back leg border with the front leg border, space 9 buttons evenly and sew in place.

Sew a button to the pocket and 3 buttons to the front opening.

Toy Bunnies

*These knitted bunnies make chic and cuddly toys, and
you can even knit your own tiny infant bunny to accompany
the adults.*

Adult
Bunny

You will need

For one adult bunny

YARN

1 x 50g/1¾oz ball of Rowan *Pure Wool DK* in
Snow 012, Enamel 013 or Shale 002 (MC)
Scraps of Rowan *Pure Wool DK* in Dew 057 (CC)
for inner ears, paws and foot pads
Scraps of black, brown or grey yarn for nose
Small amount of white or cream mohair yarn
for tail

NEEDLES

Pair of 4mm (US 6) knitting needles

EXTRAS

Kapok or other suitable toy stuffing
2 beads or buttons for eyes (if the rabbit is for
very young children be sure to fix the beads or
buttons very firmly in place or use black yarn to
embroider eyes with a large French knot, see
page 123)

A piece of cotton fabric, approx. 15 x 15cm/
6 x 6in, for fabric inner ears, paws and foot pads
Iron-on fusible interfacing, approx. 15 x 15cm/
6 x 6in
Felt, approx. 10 x 10cm/4 x 4in
Matching sewing thread

TENSION

22 sts and 30 rows to 10cm/4in square over st st
using 4mm (US 6) needles.

ABBREVIATIONS

See page 124.

FINISHED SIZE
Length approx. 27cm/10½in, excluding ears

LEGS (make 2)
Cast on 25 sts in MC.

Work 3 rows in st st.

Next row P11, sl1, P2tog, psso, P11.

Next row K10, sl1, K2tog, psso, K10.

Next row P9, sl1, P2tog, psso, P9.

Next row K8, sl1, K2tog, psso, K8. *17 sts*

Work 24 rows straight.

Cast off.

ARMS (make 2)
Cast on 12 sts in MC and cont in st st.

Inc 1 st at each end of next and foll alt row. *16 sts*

Work 19 rows in st st.

Cast off 2 sts at beg of next 2 rows. *12 sts*

Cast off 3 sts at beg of next two rows.

Cast off rem 6 sts.

BODY (make 2)
Cast on 16 sts in MC.

Work 15 rows in st st.

Dec 1 st at each end of next and every alt row until
10 sts rem.

Work 4 rows straight.

Cast off.

OUTER EARS (make 2)
Cast on 10 sts in MC.

Work 14 rows in st st.

Dec 1 st at each end of next and every foll 4th row
until 4 sts rem.

Next row P.

Next row [K2tog] twice.

Next row P2tog.

Fasten off.

LEFT CHEEK (make 1)
Cast on 10 sts in MC.

Row 1 K.

Row 2 Cast on 3 sts, P to end. *13 sts*

Row 3 Inc 1 st at each end. *15 sts*

Row 4 Inc 1 st at end of row. *16 sts*

Row 5 Inc 1 st at end of row. *17 sts*

Row 6 P to end.

Row 7 Inc 1 st at end of row. *18 sts*

Row 8 P to end.

Row 9 Inc 1 st at end of row. *19 sts*

Row 10 P to end (beg of row is nose).

Row 11 Dec 1 st at each end. *17 sts*

Row 12 Dec 1 st at beg of row, P to end. *16 sts*

Row 13 Dec 1 st at each end of row. *14 sts*

Row 14 Dec 1 st at beg of row, P to end. *13 sts*

Row 15 Dec 1 st at end of row. *12 sts*

Row 16 Dec 1 st at each end of row. *10 sts*

Row 17 Dec 1 st at each end of row. *8 sts*

Row 18 Dec 1 st at beg of row, P to end.

Cast off.

RIGHT CHEEK (make 1)
Work as for Left cheek, reversing all shaping.

CENTRE HEAD GUSSET (make 1)
Cast on 8 sts in MC.

Work 4 rows in st st.

Next row Inc 1 st at each end of next and foll alt
rows. *12 sts*

Work 17 rows.

Dec 1 st at each end of next and every foll 4th row until
2 sts rem.

Work 1 row.

Cast off.

FOOT PADS (make 2 or follow guide for fabric foot pads, paws and inner ears on page 115)

Cast on 5 sts in CC.

Work 14 rows in st st.

Cast off.

PAWS (make 2)

Cast on 5 sts in CC.

Work 7 rows in st st.

Cast off.

INNER EARS (make 2)

Cast on 8 sts in CC.

Work 12 rows in st st.

Dec 1 st at each end of next and every foll 4th row until there are 2 sts.

P2tog and fasten off.

TAIL

Make a pompom. Cut two circles of cardboard 10in/4cm diameter. Cut an inner circle 1cm/³⁄₈ in diameter in the centre of each disc. Place the two discs together, wind the mohair yarn around and through the central circle. When the inner circle is full, cut yarn. With sharp scissors, cut around the edge of the discs between the two cards. Place strong yarn between the cardboard discs and tie a firm knot, cut through the cardboard discs to release the pompom.

TO MAKE UP

For the bunny with knitted inner ears, foot pads and paws

Join the leg seam, then sew the foot pads into place and stuff.

Sew the arm seams and sew the paws in place, then stuff arms as far as the shaping.

Join the 2 sides of the body, sew the legs in place and stuff the body up to the arm shaping.

Sew the arms in place and stuff the rest of the body. Gather the neck edge.

Join the cheeks to the gusset, placing the narrow end of the gusset to the nose-end of the cheeks.

Sew the cheeks together under the chin.

Sew the inner ear to the outer ear, gather the base of the ear and sew into place. Repeat for the second ear.

Embroider the nose and the mouth.

Add beads or buttons for the eyes.

Place the pompom tail in position and sew in place.

For the bunny with fabric inner ears, foot pads and paws

Follow the making-up instructions for the knitted rabbit, substituting the following for the knitted pieces.

Using the templates (opposite) as a guide, cut 2 foot pads and 2 paws in felt and fabric.

Cut 2 inner ears in fabric, sew to the knitted outer ear as above.

Using iron-on fusible interfacing, bond the fabric foot pads and paws to the felt shapes, machine zig-zag all around each of the pieces to prevent fraying.

TEMPLATES FOR FABRIC
INNER EARS, PAWS AND FOOT PADS
(ACTUAL SIZE) – COPY AT 100%

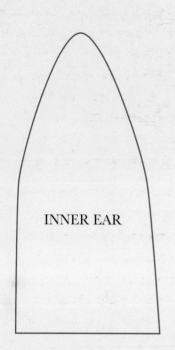

INNER EAR

PAW

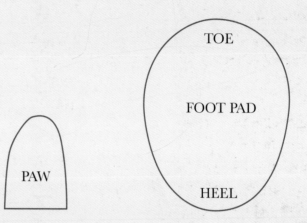

TOE

FOOT PAD

HEEL

Baby Bunny

HEAD

Using 2.5mm (US 1/2) needles and MC, cast on 15 sts.

Work 4 rows in st st.

Next row *K2, K2tog tbl, K to last 4 sts, K2tog, K2.

Work 3 rows in st st*.

Rep from * to * three times. *7 sts*

Next row K1, K2tog tbl, K2tog, K2. *5 sts*

Next row P.

Next row K2tog tbl, K1, K2tog. *3 sts*

Next row P3tog and fasten off.

BODY

Using 2.5mm (US 1/2) needles and MC, cast on 20 sts.

Work 20 rows in st st.

Next row [K2tog] to end of row. *10 sts*

Next row [P2tog] to end of row. *5 sts*

Thread yarn through rem sts and fasten off.

OUTER EAR (make 2)

Using 2.5mm (US 1/2) needles and MC, cast on 6 sts.

Beg with a K row, work 6 rows in st st.

Next row K2tog, K2, K2tog. *4 sts*

Next row P.

Next row [K2tog] twice.

Next row K2tog and fasten off.

INNER EAR (Make 2)

Using 2.5mm (US 1/2) needles and CC, cast on 5 sts.

Beg with a P row, work 5 rows in st st.

Next row K2tog, K1, K2tog.

Next row P.

Next row K.

Next row P3tog and fasten off.

TO MAKE UP

Head

Block and press work, making the head into a triangle with equal length sides.

With the cast-on edge as the lower (neck) edge, fold the three corners inward (nose) then sew up from the nose to the ear position.

Finally, sew a little way down the neck edge from the nose to form the chin, then stuff.

Body

Sew the body seam together, stuff then slip stitch the bottom edges together.

Ears

Join the inner ears to the outer ears and press.

Join the head to the body and then the ears to the head.

Using black, grey or brown yarn, embroider the nose and make a stitch for the sleeping eyes.

SHAWL

Using 4mm (US 6) needles and A, cast on 3 sts.

K 1 row.

Next row K, inc into next st, K to the last 3 sts, inc into next st, K2.

Rep the last 2 rows until there are 51 sts on the needle.

K 1 row.

Next row K2, K2tog, K to last 4 sts, K2tog tbl, K2.

Rep the last 2 rows until there are 39 sts on the needle.

Cast off.

TO MAKE UP

Block and press the shawl.

Turn the cast-off edge under and wrap the shawl around the baby bunny and sew into position.

Size Diagrams

The size diagrams show the width and length of the

finished garments.

Anmer

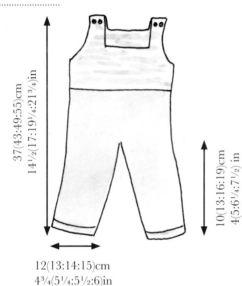

37(43:49:55)cm
14½(17:19¼:21¾)in

10(13:16:19)cm
4(5:6¼:7½)in

12(13:14:15)cm
4¾(5¼:5½:6)in

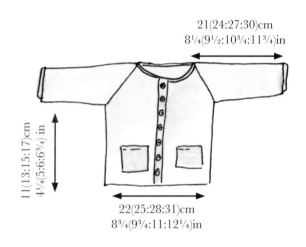

21(24:27:30)cm
8¼(9½:10¾:11¾)in

11(13:15:17)cm
4¼(5:6:6¾)in

22(25:28:31)cm
8¾(9¾:11:12¼)in

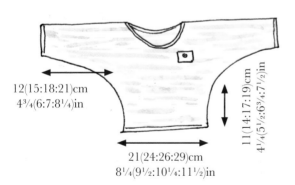

12(15:18:21)cm
4¾(6:7:8¼)in

11(14:17:19)cm
4¼(5½:6¾:7½)in

21(24:26:29)cm
8¼(9½:10¼:11½)in

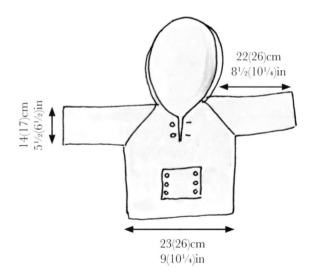

22(26)cm
8½(10¼)in

14(17)cm
5½(6½)in

23(26)cm
9(10¼)in

28(31:34:34)cm
11(12¼:13½:13½)in

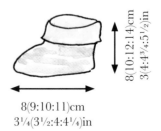

8(10:12:14)cm
3(4:4¾:5½)in

8(9:10:11)cm
3¼(3½:4:4¼)in

Balmoral

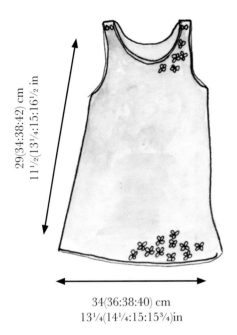

29(34:38:42) cm
11½(13¼:15:16½ in

34(36:38:40) cm
13¼(14¼:15:15¾)in

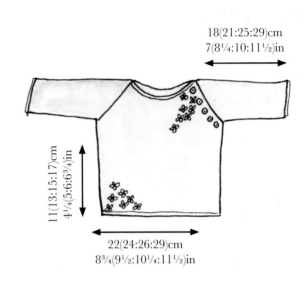

18(21:25:29)cm
7(8¼:10:11½)in

11(13:15:17)cm
4¼(5:6:6¾)in

22(24:26:29)cm
8¾(9½:10¼:11½)in

29(31:33:34)cm
11½(12¼:13:13¾)in

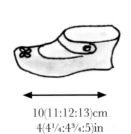

10(11:12:13)cm
4(4¼:4¾:5)in

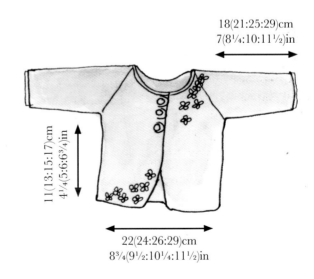

18(21:25:29)cm
7(8¼:10:11½)in

11(13:15:17)cm
4¼(5:6:6¾)in

22(24:26:29)cm
8¾(9½:10¼:11½)in

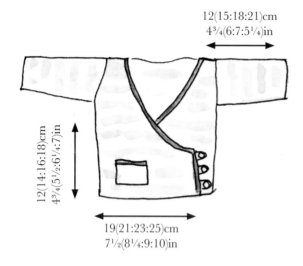

12(15:18:21)cm
4¾(6:7:5¼)in

12(14:16:18)cm
4¾(5½:6¼:7)in

19(21:23:25)cm
7½(8¼:9:10)in

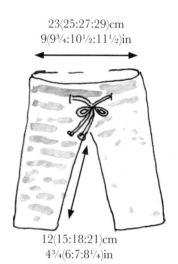

23(25:27:29)cm
9(9¾:10½:11½)in

12(15:18:21)cm
4¾(6:7:8¼)in

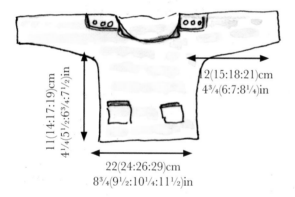

11(14:17:19)cm
4¼(5½:6¾:7½)in

12(15:18:21)cm
4¾(6:7:8¼)in

22(24:26:29)cm
8¾(9½:10¼:11½)in

25(28:31:31)cm
10(11:12¼:12¼)in

8(9:10:11)cm
3¼(3½:4:4¼)in

Sandringham

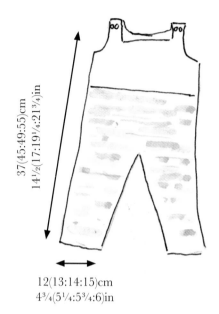

37(45:49:55)cm
14½(17:19¼:21¾)in

12(13:14:15)cm
4¾(5¼:5¾:6)in

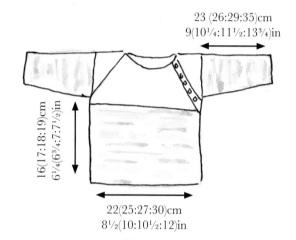

23 (26:29:35)cm
9(10¼:11½:13¾)in

16(17:18:19)cm
6¼(6¾:7:7½)in

22(25:27:30)cm
8½(10:10½:12)in

32(36:38:40)cm
12½(14:15:15¾)in

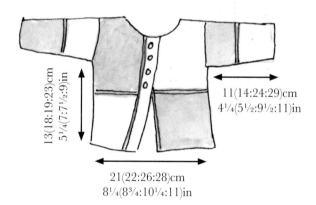

13(18:19:23)cm
5¼(7:7½:9)in

11(14:24:29)cm
4¼(5½:9½:11)in

21(22:26:28)cm
8¼(8¾:10¼:11)in

8(9:10:11)cm
3¼(3½:4:4¼)in

Windsor

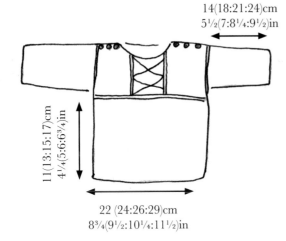

14(18:21:24)cm
5½(7:8¼:9½)in

11(13:15:17)cm
4¼(5:6:6¾)in

22 (24:26:29)cm
8¾(9½:10¼:11½)in

14(7.5:21:24)cm
5½ (7:8¼:9½)in

40(44:50:57)cm
15¾(17¼:19¼:22½)in

13(15:19:23)cm
5(6:7½:9)in

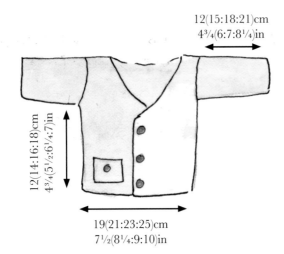

12(15:18:21)cm
4¾(6:7:8¼)in

12(14:16:18)cm
4¾(5½:6¼:7)in

19(21:23:25)cm
7½(8¼:9:10)in

25(28:31:31)cm
10(11:12¼:12¼)in

8(9:10:11)cm
3¼(3½:4:4¼)in

Embroidery Stitches

Lazy daisy & French knot

Lazy daisy stitch

Thread a yarn needle with a length of yarn. Secure the yarn on the wrong side of the knitting and bring it up at the centre of the flower. Take the needle back down at the starting point and out again at the edge of the flower, creating a loop, as shown. Secure the loop with a short stitch. Repeat to make all the petals, starting at the same central point.

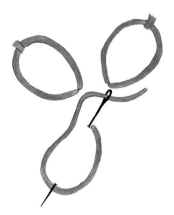

French knot

1 Thread a yarn needle with a length of yarn. Bring the needle out where the knot is required and wrap the yarn around the needle twice.

2 Push the wraps against the fabric, holding them in place with your thumb, and reinsert the needle next to where the yarn emerges.

3 Hold the knot against the fabric and take the yarn through to the back, leaving the knot in place.

Abbreviations

alt	alternate
approx.	approximately
beg	begin(s)(ning)
CC	contrast colour yarn
cm	centimetres
cont	continu(e)(ing)
dec	decreas(e)(ing)
foll	follow(s)(ing)
g	gram
in	inch(es)
inc	increas(e)(ing)
K	knit
K2tog	knit next 2 stitches together
MC	main colour yarn
M1	make one stitch by picking up horizontal loop before next stitch and knitting into back of it
P	purl
psso	pass slipped stitch over
P2tog	purl next 2 stitches together
rem	remain(s)(ing)
rep	repeat
rev st st	reverse stocking stitch / (US stockinette stitch)
RS	right side
s2kpo	slip 2 stitches together, k1, pass slipped stitches over
skpo	slip 1 stitch, k1, pass slipped stitch over
sk2po	slip 1 stitch, k2tog, pass slipped stitch over
sl 1	slip one stitch
st(s)	stitch(es)
st st	stocking stitch (1 row knit, 1 row purl)
tbl	through back of loop(s)
tog	together
WS	wrong side
yf	yarn forward
[ ]/*	repeat instructions within square brackets or between asterisks

Acknowledgements

First of all, a big thank you to Sharon Brant for that first visit to my studio and Sharon Northcott for setting the ball (or maybe that should read yarn) rolling. Thanks also to all the Brant family, especially Darren and Georgina; I certainly couldn't have done it without you! Another big thank you to my test knitters; Ann Cowling, Chris Holmes, Jacqui Daly, Elizabeth Wilson and Tina Johnson. And my superb models, William, Teo and Maddie.

Thanks also to Marilyn Wilson for translating my eclectic pattern style.

And last but by no means least, a huge thank you to Charlie Campbell – my son, my IT expert, my cheerer-upper and my friend.

Quail Publishing would also like to thank Search Press and their team, Katie French, Martin de la Bédoyère and Daniel Conway, for making this title possible.

Susan Campbell for her devotion to the project and wonderful design work.

Jesse Wilde for his wonderful photographs and patience throughout the photo shoot.

Katie Hardwicke for her thorough editing.

And finally, Rowan Yarns for their yarn support on this project

Team Quail @Quailbooks

For a complete list of all our books see

www.searchpress.com

Easy Knitted Scarves
Monica Russel
Twenty to Make

Knitted Bears
Val Pierce
20 Twenty to Make

Knitted Pirates, Princesses, Witches, Wizards & Fairies
with outfits & accessories
Annette Helfoin

Sue Stratford
Knitted Dogs & Puppies
A whole litter of fun and creative knitting patterns
Search Press

KNITTING
FOR THE
ABSOLUTE
BEGINNER
ALISON DUPERNEX

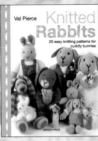

Val Pierce
Knitted Rabbits
20 easy knitting patterns for cuddly bunnies

Knitted Fairies
to cherish and charm
Fiona McDonald

Mini Christmas Knits
Sue Stratford
20 Twenty to Make

Crocheted Beanies
Frauke Kiedaisch
20 Twenty to Make

Susie Johns
Knitted Beanies
Twenty to Make

Dress up your Dolls
Lise Nymark
Sensational outfits to knit & crochet for dolls up to 45cm

CROCHET
FOR THE
ABSOLUTE
BEGINNER
PAULINE TURNER

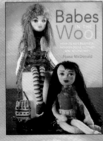

Babes in the Wool
Fiona McDonald

Mini Knitted Safari
Sachiyo Ishii

Jan Ollis
Crocheted Flowers
20 Twenty to Make

Lee Ann Garrett
Easy Knitted Tea Cosies
20 Twenty to Make

Little Bears to Knit & Crochet
Val Pierce
SEARCH PRESS

Merry Christmas Sweaters to Knit
Sue Stratford
SEARCH PRESS

Flowers to Knit and Crochet
Susie Johns & Jan Ollis
SEARCH PRESS

Baby Booties and Socks
20 Knits for Tiny Toes
SEARCH PRESS

FOLLOW US ON:
twitter
www.twitter.com/searchpress

facebook
Search Press Art and Craft Books

To request a free catalogue, go to http://www.searchpress.com/catalogues